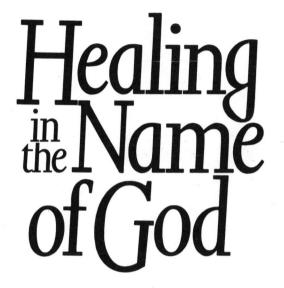

Healing in the Name of God

FAITH OR FRAUD?

Healing in the Name of God

Ted Schwarz

ZondervanPublishingHouse
Grand Rapids, Michigan

A Division of HarperCollinsPublishers

Healing in the Name of God
Copyright © 1993 by Ted Schwarz

Requests for information should be addressed to:
Zondervan Publishing House
Grand Rapids, Michigan 49530

Library of Congress Cataloging in Publication Data

Schwarz, Ted.
    Healing in the name of God : Faith or Fraud? / Ted Schwarz.
      p. cm.
    Includes bibliographical references
    ISBN 0-310-57281-9
    1. Spiritual healing. 2. Miracles. I. Title.
BT732.5.S325 1993
234'.13—dc20   92-37469
                                                          CIP

Cover design by Terry Dugan Design

Printed in the United States of America

93 94 95 96 97 98 99 00 / ML / 10 9 8 7 6 5 4 3 2 1

CONTENTS

Introduction

God is a God of miracles. From the awesome complexity of creation with its innumerable galaxies to the second-by-second pulsing of blood through our veins, God miraculously designed and sustains all of life.

I believe in miracles. I also believe that God miraculously heals people. Sometimes healing comes in spectacular ways. Doctors discover three months into Debbie's pregnancy that a lemon-sized tumor is developing on her uterus. Should they surgically remove the tumor, endangering the life of the unborn child? Or should they wait to remove the tumor until the child is born, risking the life of both mother and baby if the tumor is malignant and spreads? Debbie and her husband ask the elders of their church to pray for them—to pray for guidance and to pray for healing, if God would be so merciful. In a quiet gathering after a church service, the elders pray for John, Debbie, and the unborn child. At Debbie's next visit to the obstetrician, the ultrasound reveals that the tumor is totally gone.

Other times healing comes slowly, through the intervention of medical science and technology. Pete, a fifty-five-year-old surgeon, learns that he has a malignant tumor on his colon. Forty years ago, that diagnosis was a death warrant. But today, through the miraculous advances in surgical techniques, radiation therapy, and chemotherapy, Pete is alive and actively working in his profession. That is a miracle.

Healing isn't only physical. Healing involves the wholeness and integration of the body, mind, emotions, and spirit. For example, a couple in a church I visited just had their first baby. The father is crippled from a childhood illness, and though his mind is brilliant, his body is slightly broken. He walks with a limp, is subject to seizures when he gets too tired, and has a visual handicap. The new mother is a recovering alcoholic, who through Alcoholics Anonymous came to handle her problems constructively and eventually moved into a loving relationship, marriage, and now the joy of childbirth.

The baby daughter is perfect, healthy in both her body and mind. She is deeply loved, greatly wanted, a child who probably will never know the pain her parents endured in the years past. And if that child encounters adversity, the love with which she is surrounded will help give her the strength not only to survive but also to triumph.

To me, that family is a miracle of healing. The child represents God working in ways that humans will never be able to accomplish. Genetic engineering, in vitro fertilization, and all the other tinkering humans can do to aid in the physical birthing process can never create a situation in which two people, each broken physically or emotionally, can come together in love, uniting body, mind, and spirit, then experience healing through the creation of new life.

There are other healing miracles, of course. Spring is the healing season that follows the harsh barrenness of winter. The comforting touch of a parent heals the monsters of a small child's nightmares. A voice on the telephone heals the agony of loneliness. Enemies become friends. Peace is found in the midst of turmoil, and healing occurs. The list is endless.

Each of these examples reveals God's miraculous power to heal. The long, slow recovery is no less miraculous than the disappearing tumor. The knitting together of broken lives into a whole family is no less miraculous than a cancer that is cured.

Sometimes God heals a person without the intervention of other people. But most often he uses other people to participate in the healing, whether those other people are health-care providers, researchers, pharmacists, psychologists, or non-medical people like pastors, elders, and lay people who pray. God has uniquely gifted people like this to participate in the healing process.

I don't have trouble believing that God heals people. What troubles me deeply is the shape of contemporary faith healing. In my experience as a journalist and researcher, I have seen things that disturb me. I have seen what I consider to be abuses in the name of God. People who use the name of God to promise instant cures to anyone who will send in money to support the healer's ministry. The television personalities who orchestrate healings for their audiences. The evangelist who claims that if you put your hand on the radio, your illness will leave. The healers who travel from town to town putting on crusades that promise to heal people from all diseases.

A couple of years ago I appeared on one of the largest Christian television shows in the nation. The host, a well-known evangelist with a large following, told his audience that Jesus was working in their midst. As he spoke of a heart condition being cured, an excited elderly man in the audience turned to his wife and said aloud, "Martha, he's talking about me. He knows about my heart. He knows I'm going to be healed. He said my name, Martha."

The wife, happy with her husband yet embarrassed by his outburst, took his hand and squeezed it, trying to quiet him at the same time that they shared this "miracle." After the show ended, I watched them go to the evangelist and thank him for bringing this miracle healing into the man's life.

The evangelist never bothered to mention the fact that he had *not* given a name when he made his statement about the healing of a heart. In fact, most likely several people in the audience had been diagnosed with one heart problem or another, since it's a common ailment in our society.

But this man had reacted as if a personal healing had occurred. He expressed immediate happiness and peace. He spoke aloud, causing the studio audience to gasp in delight, thrilled for this healing, while one of the camera operators swung the lens in his direction to capture his elation for the viewing audience. And the evangelist stood clasping the man's hand, tears at the corners of his eyes, humbly confessing to being just a path for God's healing power. The evangelist did nothing, he explained. God did everything. Yet it was made very clear to the couple that God had done his work through the evangelist—to whom they gave a check before leaving the studio.

There were other reactions in the audience, less dramatic than the man's outburst. One woman smiled and clutched her wrist. Her hand bore some of the distortions that occur when joints are damaged by arthritis. And a man who had his leg propped on the chair next to him flexed his leg a bit and looked hopeful.

Yet the evangelist had said nothing. He spoke in vague generalities and let the emotions of the audience create an image of an event that might or might not have occurred. And when the show was over, if someone like the couple wanted to thank him for his "cure," he was more than happy to accept thanks for his role. He was also quite happy to accept the money necessary to continue "God's work."

This is not to say that the evangelist is not a Christian. He may have truly had faith in his own pronouncements. I have no idea, because when I tried to get to the couple, to take their names, to arrange to follow up on this healing after the man had a chance to go to a doctor, the publicist for the evangelist and one of the security guards quickly ushered me to a different room. "We never disturb the members of our audience," I was told.

I explained, "I just wanted to arrange to follow up on this healing, to be able to write about what we all witnessed today. Perhaps you would be willing to give them my card, to give them the chance to call me collect if they choose. That way they won't feel I'm invading their privacy. I won't know who they are or how to reach them, but they'll be able to contact me."

"That won't be possible," I was told.

"Then how do you know what has taken place? We wouldn't know of the healing powers of Jesus if men such as Matthew, Mark, and Luke hadn't written of the events. And Luke was a physician, so his witness was all the more important. I just want the chance to tell others."

The publicist became quite solemn. "We never know how long these healings will last," she said. "You saw God's work today. That man is in perfect health, even though he came here quite sick. But we know nothing about him. He might leave here and let Satan get hold of him. His heart condition could return in an hour, a day, a week. He might go to the doctor and be worse than before he came to the show.

"That doesn't mean he wasn't healed. It only means that his faith is too weak to sustain the miracle. You might talk with him after Satan has taken hold and find that his doctor has told him he's still sick. You could have Satan cause you to question what you witnessed here with your own eyes. Without meaning to do so, you could do the work of Satan by writing about what you will come to think was a false miracle."

"But the man might be a good Christian," I argued. "He might have conquered the influence of Satan all of his life and now be impervious to attacks of evil. His witness and his doctor's corroboration of what occurred today could be an important message I could write about for others. It would show another triumph of God through . . ."

"I'm sorry," she interrupted. "It's policy." Then she left, the security guard remaining in the room with me and some of the other guests from the show until the audience had departed the area.

"No sense in being mobbed," we were told.

No sense in risking our talking with people from the audience, I suspected.

These disturbing events have forced me to ask a lot of questions:

- Is faith healing legitimate?
- Are faith healers legitimate?
- What does the Bible say about healing?
- What does it mean if a person is not healed?
- What role does the ill person's faith play in the healing?
- Is this kind of healing new to our society?
- What makes people go to faith healers?
- What responsibility do healers have to the people who come to them?
- How can we discern the fraudulent healer from the person genuinely gifted by God to heal?

This book is the outcome of those questions. I do not presume to have found all of the answers. Many of them I must leave in the hands of theologians, philosophers, and medical people more competent than I. Most of them I leave in the hands of a sovereign God, who knows all things and understands the things that remain mysteries to us.

But I will share with you some of the conclusions I have reached through my research and interviews with people involved in faith healing. My hope is that these reflections and conclusions will help you discern the genuine healers from the frauds. In addition, I hope that this will lead all of us to hold the fraudulent healers accountable for what they do in the name of God.

Part I
Healing and Healers

1

Whom Do You Trust?

What would you have thought if I had begun this book in the following way?

I feel a miracle happening right now. As you hold this book, God is working in your life. There is healing taking place. Miraculous healing. The hand of Jesus is coming through these pages, bringing hope, health, happiness.

I sense someone out there, maybe you, maybe a friend or neighbor, being healed of heart disease right this moment. Perhaps the person is unaware of the problem. Perhaps the person feels in perfect health, even though he or she was about to be struck down with the pain and devastation of a heart attack. In fact, if that person had seen a doctor just a moment ago, he or she would have been rushed to a hospital where teams of surgeons would have been waiting to replace the valves, bypass the arteries, perhaps transplant the entire organ.

But not anymore. God's hand reached out through this book and caused a healing. If that person now goes to see the doctor, the doctor will say, "You're in perfect health. I don't know why you even came to me. Why, your heart is as strong as that of an athlete twenty years younger."

And we can smile at the thought, can't we? We can smile because we know the truth. That person was sick, and now that person is well. And the reason is because of this book and Doctor Jesus!

I feel other miracles taking place. It's not just one healing that's happening. I can feel a cancer being cured. I can sense someone who has lived with painful arthritis now feeling comfort, moving his fingers with greater ease than he has known in years.

I can feel Doctor Jesus at work wherever this book is sold, whenever this book is touched. God's miracle of healing is coming to you by way of this publisher, so go out and buy more copies. Buy copies for friends, for loved ones, for strangers on the street. Fill your living room with extra books because you never know when you will want to pass on this miracle of healing.

Yes, buy this book. Restore your health. And, incidentally, make me very rich. After all, my bank balance isn't healthy, and if you will just have the faith necessary to buy $100 worth of these books, $1,000 worth of these books, $10,000 worth of these books, then, praise the Lord, my bank balance will be healed!

Would you trust me?

Some of you would read such an introduction and become angry. You would think I was a blasphemer or an outrageous charlatan. But some of you might think something else, at least until I told you to spend as much money as possible acquiring more books. Some of you might have thought that maybe, just maybe, this book would be the instant answer to whatever problems afflict you.

You would have reason for such a belief, after all. The publisher of this book is a well-respected religious publishing company. I am a widely published author, whose works appear in both secular and religious bookstores. Many people believe that because of this, I couldn't say that I had the power to heal unless it were true. After all, isn't this book about faith healing? And isn't it possible that despite the cynical manner in which I might have written such an opening, I may be an unknowing vehicle for God's healing powers?

Look at the Old Testament prophets. They were all "unlikely vessels." Few of them were eloquent speakers. None of them came from the ranks of the high born, and many were neither educated nor articulate. Even Moses, who was adopted into a life of wealth and privilege, was essentially an outcast who was so tongue-tied that he needed his brother, Aaron, to speak for him.

Perhaps I'm too modest. Perhaps I *am* God's unlikely vessel, his reluctant prophet, a man whose touch can heal in ways I don't realize. Perhaps, even as you read this, a healing is taking place in your life, a miracle, a . . .

Seductive isn't it? If we can just encounter someone who has that special power—a preacher, a teacher, a doctor, or even a street-corner evangelist with the fire of faith burning in his or her soul—all our problems will be solved.

We want to be healed by magic. We want to put our trust in the false gods with the gift of gab, the pious words, and just the right tone of voice for us to feel that here, indeed, is God's anointed. Tragically, there are many men and women who will fill that role.

GOD'S "ANOINTED"

The opening paragraphs of this chapter are actually a paraphrase of a technique that is common among some television evangelists and some ministers with extremely large congregations. They make vague statements and rely on the sheer volume of listeners to get a reaction they desire.

If I have five thousand people in front of me—males and females, young and old, people from several ethnic and racial groups—the chances are good that among this diverse group of people will be those experiencing the most common ailments in our society: heart disease, cancer, and degenerative joint problems such as arthritis. Statistics tell us that overweight men who have passed the age of forty are statistically at high risk for heart attack, as are obese women a few years past menopause. Assembly-line workers, typists, computer operators, and laborers who regularly lift and move heavy objects all are likely to have arthritis or carpal tunnel syndrome. Outdoor workers and people who spend extensive time exposed to the sun have a high risk of skin cancer. Add such additional risk factors as smoking or exposure to pollutants and the chance of having cancer increases many times. And if elderly people are in my audience, many of them will have vision problems.

These are facts, statistics carefully developed through extensive studies by health organizations. And the facts are frequently mentioned in news magazines, the feature sections of newspapers, on radio and television talk shows.

Honest people know this. And the men and women who want to take advantage of the public are also aware of such facts. However, the latter are the ones who frequently use vague allusions to convey the truth.

My experience on the television show was not unique. "Healing" sessions like the one I witnessed appear on a regular basis, using tricks that help convince others of their greatness.

PEOPLE GIFTED TO HEAL

Does that mean all healers are to be suspect? Are all healers frauds? No. Some people are gifted to heal.

The list of spiritual gifts described in 1 Corinthians 12 includes the "gifts of healing." The people gifted by God to heal may include not only those people who participate in healing through prayer and other spiritual, non-medical means but also the full range of medical professionals. For the purposes of this book, let's limit our focus to the faith healer—the man or woman who facilitates the healing process through faith in God, without the intervention of medicine, using prayer, anointing with oil, the laying on of hands, slaying in the Spirit, or any combination of these non-medical procedures.

How can you tell the genuine faith healer from the fraud? How will you know if a faith healer is a person gifted by God to heal? Legitimate faith healers expect success yet recognize that they have no idea what shape the healing may take or when it may occur. They know that God can grow a new hand on the arm of a machinist who lost it in an industrial accident, for example. They also know that God may choose to not do so, indeed seldom has done so, and that the machinist may go through life with a prosthesis instead. They see healing in three forms—the miraculous we understand, the miraculous beyond comprehension, and the internal (spiritual/psychological) healing.

A *miraculous healing we understand* involves medical knowledge used to cure someone of heart problems, cancer, or an illness such as pneumonia. We have learned to put together what might be considered the pieces of a puzzle—medication, a surgical procedure, inhalation therapy, physical therapy, and all the other tools we have learned to help the body recover. We are working with God's creation as we have learned to do, being allowed in a tiny way to share in his miraculous healing powers. Yet our understanding is from God, and the basic tools, the billions of cells, the innumerable particles of matter that comprise the human body are all his, all beyond our ability to duplicate.

The legitimate faith healer knows that God most often chooses to heal diseases through medical science and medical professionals. The faith healer does not diminish the importance of these God-given means or deride the medical profession.

A *miraculous healing beyond comprehension* is the healing that occurs when "irreversible" medical conditions are reversed. The person whose body is so wasted that death seems inevitable rallies, heals, and returns to normal life. The inoperable cancer goes into remission for so many years that the person dies from the ravages of old age, not from the disease. The malignant tumor on the lung disappears. We witness the hand of God without human involvement other than through faith expressed in prayer for the ill person.

Internal healing comes when the afflicted person finds peace with a life that may not be the kind he or she anticipated. Louise, who has advanced multiple sclerosis, believes that God can heal physical diseases. Three times she has met with her church's elders and prayer counselors, who anointed her with oil and prayed for a complete healing. Louise's symptoms did not recede; in fact her condition worsened—at least physically.

However, Louise experienced a deep inner healing— an incomprehensible peace and acceptance of her illness. Her anxiety was replaced by joy that spilled over to everyone she met. Her pain is still very real; she copes with it every day. But God's grace has touched her so deeply that she lives with the pain and the degeneration of her body with grace and calm. People around her are amazed at her ability to be joyful, mentally productive, and active in serving the Lord despite her severe illness. She says of her life, "God has chosen not to heal me of my physical disease, but that no longer matters to me. What matters is that he promises to be with me *in the midst* of my suffering. That's all I need. And maybe that is the greater miracle."

This internal healing, one that finds God's grace to live through and in the experience, is as miraculous as a physical recovery. There is an acceptance of self, of life, of the eternal that comes through counseling, prayer, meditation, or however else God reaches out to the person. The body may still be broken, but the afflicted person is healed, his or her spirit soaring with the eagles.

Genuine faith healers can accept healing on all three levels. They understand the place of healing through medical science. They accept the mystery of God's choosing to heal through non-medical ways. And they accept that people for whom they have prayed may not recover physically from their illness. They are not threatened by that possibility. They leave the ultimate decision in God's hands, knowing that his ways are beyond human understanding. Fraudulent faith healers have a hard time if the person is not healed. These healers will blame the ill person's lack of faith or try to convince the ill person that he or she *is* healed, even if the symptoms of the illness persist. (More about these issues in later chapters.)

Genuine faith healers do not tie the healing process to money or to personal fame. They truly see themselves as tools that God uses in mysterious ways. Their focus is on God alone, not on themselves or their reputation. Rarely will genuine faith healers involve themselves in the platform show that conjures up a healing mystique, a dynamic that manipulates or controls the audience.

The next few chapters will take a look at several faith healers, examining the questionable practices of some of them.

2

The Healers

For centuries cultures have looked to certain people—healers—to cure them of diseases and ailments. Who are these healers? What makes them unique? This chapter will look at several biblical healers as well as two contemporary healers. Later, chapter 7 will take an historical look at people who had the healing touch.

GOD, THE HEALER

An Old Testament story illustrates how people saw God as the healer. In 2 Kings 5 we read the story of Naaman, an Aramean army captain who had leprosy. Naaman's Israeli servant girl boldly suggests, "If only [you] would see the prophet who is in Samaria! He would cure [you] of [your] leprosy" (5:3).

After consulting with his boss, the king of Aram, Naaman travels to Israel and reports to the Israeli king, who panics, "Am I God? Can I kill and bring back to life? Why does [the king of Aram] send someone to me to be cured of his leprosy?" (5:7). When Elisha the prophet hears of the king's distress, he invites Naaman to come to see him.

Naaman arrives at Elisha's house with great anticipation. But Elisha doesn't even come out of the house to greet the army captain. Instead, he sends a servant to instruct Naaman, "Go, wash yourself seven times in the Jordan, and your flesh will be restored and you will be cleansed" (5:10).

Naaman was outraged. Here he had come a great distance for a serious healing, and the prophet, who never even shows his face, tells him to wash in a muddy river. What a hoax! Naaman complains, "I thought that he would surely come out to me and stand and call on the name of the Lord his God, wave his hand over the spot and cure me of my leprosy. Are not . . . the rivers of Damascus better than any of the waters of Israel? Couldn't I wash in them and be cleansed?" (5:11–12).

But Naaman's servants settle him down and encourage him to obey the prophet's instructions. Naaman washes seven times in the Jordan River and his leprosy disappears. "His flesh was restored and became clean like that of a young man" (5:14).

Amazed by the results of his obedience to what seemed like ludicrous instructions, Naaman exclaims, "Now I know that there is no God in all the world except in Israel" (5:15).

This story reveals several interesting dynamics. First, the young Israeli servant knew of God's power to heal, and she may have known that God had used Elisha as an instrument of healing in other circumstances. She had enough faith in God and the healing process to risk her job by suggesting that Naaman go to see Elisha.

Second, when Naaman arrived in Israel, he went to the

king. The king's immediate response indicated that he somehow felt responsible to heal this foreign army captain. There seems to be a cultural expectation that the king would be the person to bring about the healing. (In chapter 7 we'll examine this phenomenon of the "royal touch" more carefully.) But the king panics. He knows he has no healing power, and he suspects he's being set up.

Third, Elisha hears of the encounter between Naaman and the king, and he intervenes, inviting the captain to see him. When Naaman arrives at Elisha's doorstep, however, Elisha doesn't even come out to greet the man—a gesture very uncharacteristic of Middle Eastern cultures. Instead, he sends word through a servant for Naaman to wash seven times in the Jordan River, an unconventional set of instructions, to say the least. Elisha's instructions do not meet Naaman's expectations: he thought Elisha would examine his illness, pray, and wave his hand over the leprous spot. And because Elisha doesn't meet Naaman's expectations, Naaman rejects the instructions in disgust, wondering why he ever had traveled so far to see this inept man. But in the end, Naaman's servants convince him to obey Elisha's instructions. And Naaman is healed.

Fourth, the end result of the healing is that Naaman declares his faith in God as the only true God in all the world. He saw God, not Elisha, as the healer. Naaman recognized divine intervention; he knew that the water of the Jordan River had no healing power.

CHRIST, THE MASTER HEALER

When many people think of a healer, they think of the master healer, Jesus Christ. Christ healed in a variety of ways. Sometimes he touched the person. Other times he spoke a word. Sometimes he used methods that seem unconventional to us—like putting spittle on a blind man's eye—but were understandable in the culture of that day.

A major part of Christ's three-year ministry involved healing—bringing people into physical, mental, spiritual wholeness. A brief survey of Luke's gospel alone reveals a wide range of healing miracles. In the early days of his public ministry, Christ healed Peter's mother-in-law's fever with a "rebuke" (4:39). Later on that same day Jesus laid his hands on many people who were brought to him with various kinds of sickness and healed them (4:40).

Christ touched the untouchable leper who came asking for healing, and immediately the leprosy left the man (5:13). When some men lowered their paralytic friend through a hole in the roof of the house in which Jesus was teaching, Christ forgave the paralytic's sin and healed the man of his paralysis (5:17–26). In response to the faith of a centurion, Jesus healed the man's servant, without ever saying a word, seeing the sick servant, or touching him (7:1–10). With a word Christ brought to life the dead son of a widow on whom he had compassion (7:11–17). He healed a deranged man by casting out demons that had taken over the man's body (8:26–39).

A woman who had been afflicted by twelve years of hemorrhaging touched Jesus' cloak, and her bleeding immediately stopped (8:40–48). Moments later Jesus took the hand of the dead daughter of a synagogue leader and brought her back to life (8:49–56). Later he placed his hands on a woman who had been crippled for eighteen years, and she straightened up (13:10–13). During a trip to Jerusalem, ten leprous men called out to Jesus, who merely told them to go show themselves to the priests; when the men obeyed Christ's instructions, they were cleansed (17:11–14). In response to the calling out of a blind beggar who sat by the side of the road, Christ asked the man, "What do you want me to do for you?" When the blind man asked for his sight, Jesus responded, "Receive your sight; your faith has healed you" (18:35–43); the man immediately regained his sight. During his arrest before his trial and crucifixion, Jesus touched the head of a servant whose ear had been cut off in the fracas; the servant's ear was healed (22:50–51).

In his healing ministry Christ recognized the faith of people who came to him and challenged that faith to grow. His goal was not to call attention to himself but to point the healed people to God's power.

HEALERS IN THE EARLY CHURCH

After Jesus' death, resurrection, and ascension, God empowered the leaders of the early church to heal. The book of Acts tells us that the apostle Peter healed a crippled beggar. When the beggar asked Peter for money, he said, "Silver or gold I do not have, but what I have I give you. In the name of Jesus Christ of Nazareth, walk." The man instantly was cured of his crippled condition and jumped to his feet (Acts 3:1–10). As the early church grew, many people took their sick friends and relatives to the apostles for healing. Acts 5:16 tells us that "all of them were healed."

As the early church developed, the responsibility for healing broadened to the body of elders responsible for the spiritual direction of each church. In his letter to the churches, James gives clear instructions for how the church should deal with sick people: "Is any one of you sick? He should call the elders of the church to pray over him and anoint him with oil in the name of the Lord. And the prayer offered in faith will make the sick person well; the Lord will raise him up. If he has sinned, he will be forgiven. Therefore confess your sins to each other and pray for each other so that you may be healed. The prayer of a righteous man is powerful and effective" (James 5:14–16).

According to James, the first step when a church member is ill is to call for the elders of the church. Before this time, elders were responsible for directing the affairs of the church, guarding the church from error, and shepherding the people of God the way a shepherd tended the lambs. But here the elders were to take on a new function. They were expected to pray for the sick and anoint them with oil.[1] They were acting as functioning ministers to members of the congregation.

James even defines how the prayers should be given. The prayer should be "offered in faith"—essentially as an accomplished fact, completely without doubt about whether or not it will work.

CONTEMPORARY HEALERS

Healing continues in the church today. Healing services come in many shapes and sizes. I have attended charismatic Catholic gatherings that used the laying on of hands for cancer healing, followed by prayer by a group that was engaged in regular intercessory prayer. I have been to storefront churches where a small group led by a preacher who earned his living as a janitor had special healing nights during which prayers were said for the afflicted. I have attended revival ceremonies, some led by nationally known charismatics, others by newly called people just getting their feel of how to preach. And I have been to the Order of St. Luke, whose members include Episcopalians, Lutherans, and Methodists, and whose ceremonies are conservative.

With the advent of mass media, healing ministries have undergone a change. Healings that once were done in the privacy of a small group that knew the sick person have been replaced by healings called forth in meetings of hundreds and sometimes thousands of people. Or the healings are done over the radio waves or the television screen.

Let's look more closely at two contemporary healers, Oral Roberts and Ernest Angley. These men represent two of the many schools of thought in contemporary faith healing.

Oral Roberts

Among the faith healers who have a public ministry is Oral Roberts. Few people are neutral when it comes to reacting to Oral Roberts' words and deeds. They adore him, seeing him as God's messenger, or they revile him, seeing him as one who may be preying on the vulnerable. Roberts is not the leader of some cult but a minister in the mainstream United Methodist Church.

Oral Roberts, according to physicians who have worked with him, truly believes in holistic (or wholistic) healing. He understands that mental attitudes, self-hate, self-doubt, the stress of being an adult victim of child abuse, and other factors can all affect a person's health. He also believes in the peace that can come from God and the healing knowledge of physicians. He is comfortable with surgery, psychiatry, and all the other branches of healing in combination with prayer, the laying on of hands, and similar methods of faith healing.

The problem, according to the physicians who were willing to be interviewed, is that Oral Roberts does not use the vocabulary of the doctors and psychiatrists. Instead of talking about hysteric dissociation, for example, he will refer to the "demon of child abuse." On the one hand he will encourage the physicians to use traditional methods of treating cancer, like chemotherapy and radiation therapy, along with prayer and stress counseling, but he will talk of the "demon of cancer." Oral Roberts actually was one of the first faith healers to be comfortable with all paths to healing, even though he believes that nothing would be possible without the will and love of God.

Oral Roberts' language, coupled with what many feel may be exaggerated claims of some of his experiences, stop many people from carefully examining his work. They would rather not have to deal with the gray area that dominates much of the work of religious healers.

Yet there have been changes, changes often overlooked by his early critics. This has nothing to do with his fund-raising efforts but rather his philosophy about healing.

In 1986, Oral Roberts began writing in a manner that fits the beliefs of a growing number of mainstream healers—physicians, psychiatrists, and others. He began stressing the concept of holism—of treating the body, the mind, and the spirit—though he did not use the language of those who are involved in the holistic movement. In his book *Your Road to Recovery,* Roberts wrote:

> How much health do you want to have?
> Specifically.
> You may say, "Well, I just want to be healthy."
> How healthy? There are different degrees of being healthy. Do you just want to be free of a particular disease or pain in your body? Or do you want to really have fine health? Are you willing to lose the extra pounds and exercise in the right ways to have the greatest amount of health you can possibly have? Are you willing to quit smoking or give up other bad health habits in order to get God's best health for you?
> How much health do you want to have?[2]

Roberts addresses both personal responsibility and the power of God, recognizing that humans can't be self-abusive, then demand a miracle through faith. Roberts believes that God can heal anyone of anything. Yet he also recognizes human will, the ability of the ill person to be a participant in the health process. More important, he recognizes the necessity of individual action in conjunction with prayer to receive fully what God has to offer.

For example, Roberts talks about how God gives us the ability to make changes. He shows that if someone is suffering in a particular climate because of the cold, the humidity, allergy, pollutants, or some other factor, that person has the ability to relocate to avoid a negative stress from the environment.

Likewise we can change jobs, change our diet, increase or alter our exercise patterns, get more sleep, or do whatever else is necessary to provide the framework for better health. God is on our side no matter what we do, but we also have a responsibility. We choose to what degree we are working with God for the best possible life.

Ernest Angley

A contemporary faith healer whom some people believe uses guilt in his healing practices is Ernest Angley. In his book *Faith in God Heals the Sick,* he writes:

> Accept God's Word through faith. Symptoms of your disease may recur after you are prayed for, but never let those symptoms cause you to doubt what God has done for you.
>
> Do not look back! Lot's wife looked back and lost her life. You, too, will lose yours if you turn back to your city of bondage, the sickness and despair where the devil has held you in captivity. Don't look back to the horrible condition you were in, but look forward to a new life—a life free from sin and sickness.[3]

Angley states, "Remember, sickness is the work of the devil. . . ."[4] He also warns that God is intolerant of any deviation. For example, Angley has written, "A young man born deaf and mute came into the healing line. He had never uttered one word in his life. God healed him that night, and he could hear and speak; but a few nights later he got drunk. Because of it, he not only lost his hearing, but the mute spirit re-entered and took his powers of speech."[5]

The closest Angley has come to the holistic concept of Roberts is when he stresses that an individual must give up bad habits either to be healed or to stay healed. "You certainly cannot smoke, chew tobacco, use snuff, drink intoxicating drinks or use dope for the glory of God," he stresses.[6]

The Two Styles

The differences in messages are subtle, but they create quite disparate attitudes among the followers. Oral Roberts does not see God as waiting to strike down someone who makes a mistake or has problems.[7] He shows that the degree of health one achieves is determined by both God's blessing and personal action.

Angley, on the other hand, represents God as far more stern and demanding. There is little tolerance for failure, and a person who has a relapse has obviously sinned. By Roberts' reasoning, a person who lives in Minnesota and is troubled with arthritis in the harsh cold of winter, should be able to pray to God for healing, dress warmly, and move to a climate where the winters are mild. Angley, on the other hand, leaves the impression that the healing should not require anything more than faith. The person need not move. In fact, it could be argued that such a move would show only partial faith.

Angley also uses examples that are either inaccurate or inappropriate to the message. Lot's wife, fleeing from Sodom, disobeyed the Lord's statement not to look back at the city under destruction and died. Some people might argue that her curiosity caused her death. Others would say it was her disobedience to God. But either way, the fact that she turned into a pillar of salt had nothing to do with faith in God's healing power.

Likewise, while the vast majority of clergy would agree that excessive use of drugs or alcohol is destructive, Angley's writing implies that any use of intoxicants is bad. This message is a harsh one, not only for those groups who use wine for communion (Catholics, Episcopalians, Lutherans, and others), but also when applied to Jesus and his mother, Mary, who enjoyed wine at a wedding feast (John 2:1–11). The message of the story is not that drinking wine is good or bad, for Jesus doesn't condemn it and he respects his mother's wish that he supply more wine than was available. Yet Angley's writing, taken literally, appears to condemn any use of intoxicants. As a result, it could be construed that someone who experiences a healing and then takes communion in a church where wine is offered could return to ill health.

Both Angley and Roberts stress healing ministries. But where Roberts' statements reflect a belief that someone can be healed by God and remain troubled by not following proper health-care practices, Angley is more likely to say that someone who is not healed has sinned. Illness, and especially a relapse, reflects the failing of the ill person.

My goal at this point is not to discuss the role faith plays in the healing process; chapter 4 will do that more fully. Rather, I have tried to paint a portrait of two contemporary faith healers and the issues surrounding each healer.

PROFESSIONAL FAITH HEALERS

Let me discuss for a moment another group of healers, a group I call the professional faith healers. These healers travel from place to place, staying in one area only a few days or a week. Healing crusades or healing meetings are their "bread and butter."

If I seem cynical about such faith healers, it's because

I've seen them at work, and I have trouble believing all of what I see. The professional healer is an on-stage person, well behaved, impeccably groomed, articulate, confident, telling stories of miracles worked in Cleveland, Anchorage, New York, Chicago, Houston, or wherever. The miracles happened there because the posters, the handbills, and the advertisements all say they happened, because the advance workers and even the healer all say they happened.

Not that I can check them, you understand. Names are seldom given, and even when they are, I am not expected to be so lacking in faith that I place telephone calls to check out the miracles proclaimed. The professional faith healer never has to answer for what is said, never has to get involved following the healing.

Professional faith healers regularly speak of their past successes as proof of what they have accomplished. Healing crusades often include testimonials from people who may be part of the staff or people who claimed to have been healed by the faith healer. Usually the healed people have no medical evidence of the healing, and some never had medical evidence of a problem.

A woman who stands in front of an audience to say she was healed from a heart problem may never have been diagnosed with a heart problem. Instead, she may have been suffering from a muscle strain on the left side of her body or a broncho-spasm caused by stress, including the stress from smoking or air pollution.

A man who has been diagnosed with a lung problem goes to the faith healer and believes he has been healed. He never goes to have follow-up medical care to determine if the lung problem has in fact disappeared. He gives testimony to his healing without ever knowing if it in fact really happened.

Whatever the case, giving testimony concerning the cure reinforces the miracle they feel they have experienced.

And if they are again troubled with some of the discomfort they faced earlier, their testimony should reinforce the reality of the healing.

Professional faith healers' testimonies about personal success will vary from individual to individual. Some claim to have raised the dead, giving themselves a direct link to Jesus. Others tell of the standard Christian miracles—the blind see, the lame walk, the deaf hear.

Professional faith healers frequently ridicule doctors and the medical profession. The faith healer will talk about the elderly widow the doctors in the nursing home had written off as too near death to be saved. Or the doctors took one look at their X-rays and said that nothing would save the person. Or the doctors wanted to cut off a withered limb oozing green pus—until the healer laid his hands on the arm, called on the healing power of Jesus to come through his body, and the arm returned to normal.

A standard technique is to remind the audience of previous healings, even though most of the audience are new to the gathering and did not witness the healing. "You remember two weeks ago when I cured (or "the Lord cured") the blind man? He's driving a car for the first time in his life." Or the talk will be of the grapefruit-sized cancer tumor that shriveled up and disappeared after "I commanded it to heal." Or the healer will refer to the man whose short leg grew three inches.

Sometimes the miracles seem plausible. Sometimes they seem outlandish. But they are rarely challenged. The audience members who were present at the time assume that they missed seeing the special miracle because of the crush of the crowd. Those who were not present join in the shouts of "Amen" and "Hallelujah" because such rejoicing seems appropriate.

Professional Healer vs. the Local Pastor

What disturbs me about the professional healers and their healing services is that these healers are accountable to no one. Looking at it from that perspective, the pastor and elders of a person's local church seem to me to be a better place to look for healing prayer.

What appeals to me about the healing services I've attended in neighborhood churches is that in each service, the person who acted as pastor, priest, or leader was also the church members' regular caretaker. This was the man or woman who prayed with them in the hospitals and funeral homes, who delighted in the ceremonies involving baptism, communion, weddings, and other rites of passage. This was the person who had seen their joy and their grief, who had heard their most overwhelming problems and been made aware of their most embarrassing or crippling fears. This was their friend, adviser, confidant—their shepherd and teacher, their nurturer, ethicist, and moral guide. In short, the leader was an integral part of the membership, and in many cases an integral part of the community.

This gives a built-in accountability to the situation. If such a person makes healing claims that sound exaggerated or miraculous, you can call the person involved and ask what happened. After all, you know each other and are part of the same church and community. If the minister is lying, you'll know it soon enough.

With the professional healer, however, you have no way of verifying the truth of his or her claims. The healer is an on-stage person, removed from the daily lives of the people who have come for healing. The healer is often slick, well rehearsed, giving the impression that it's all a show. The healer may truly believe in God's power to heal, but the assumption is that God needs a ringmaster to orchestrate the show, calling out instructions, making it all happen.

I'm uncomfortable with that setting, and so is the

Pittsburgh minister who tells the following story. He and I were on a television program in Philadelphia together, and after the show we were discussing the problems of traveling professional healers. He agreed to let me quote him if I didn't use his name because he was concerned with the possible reaction of his parishioners. "We had a healing service at our church, and one of our sweetest parishioners came forward. She was a pillar of the community, in her early seventies. But her life had been hard, and she was battling cancer. She had been on our prayer list for many months, and I spent a lot of time with her in the hospital, in the convalescent home, and in her own apartment. Sometimes she wanted to read with me from the Bible. Sometimes she wanted to pray. And sometimes she just wanted to do what she called 'gossip,' though it was never malicious. It was always trying to identify the needs of the congregation and people she knew from the community, then see what she or I or the members could do to help.

"We had a laying on of hands, and this woman seemed to glow in the Spirit when we touched her. She radiated a love for her Maker, a trust . . . it deeply moved all of us. I thought we were witnessing a miracle, but her cancer just kept spreading, killing her a couple of months later.

"She was at peace, of course. She was always at peace with the realities of life and death, with pain and pleasure.

"But the woman's daughter became a little unhinged. She accused me of being a charlatan, of taking advantage of her mother for money. She thought her mother should have been in bed, resting, instead of puttering around the church whenever we needed volunteers for something.

" 'I told Mother to go to a *real* healer. I offered to send her to one of those television preachers who really work miracles,' the daughter said to me. 'But, no. She was too much under your influence,' she said bitterly.

"There was no reasoning with her grief. The daughter

wasn't a member of our church and didn't trust me or any other member of our church.

"Ironically, I once was present when the mother and daughter had gotten into an argument about this. I had been sitting at the house, reading the Bible with my parishioner, when she told her daughter that she was healed. I still remember her words—'My body's worn out, but my soul's at peace with the Lord. I'm ready for whatever he has for me to do next. You can't be more healed than that!'

"She also asked her daughter, 'Which of those television healers would come by the house, would visit me in the hospital, would telephone to make certain I was doing all right? I can't be healed sitting on my butt in front of a television set,' the mother said. 'God can touch my heart. God can give me the tools to change my life. But I've got to be *with others* to follow his way, not sitting alone in front of that screen.'

"Yes, that dear woman taught me a lot. But I can still hear the daughter's angry words. She wanted to send her mother to the big leagues, not some church where she knew some of the elders from the time they were kids, teasing each other, calling each other names, wearing torn clothing, and dripping their ice cream all over their T-shirts. It was as if the big-name faith healers never were quite human, as if their homes were probably without bathrooms and kitchens because they had no need of either."

The Show

Again, I may seem cynical when I refer to the healing services of professional healers as a show, but what I have seen and what I have been told has led me to be suspicious of much of what goes on in these services.

First, there is the act of advance publicity. This means far more than announcing past healings. It is a method for convincing people that miracles and healings can occur on the healer's time frame. The local clergy may hold healing services, but miracles seem rare or slow in coming. Laying on of hands and intercessory prayer may be a part of Jack Williams' colon cancer treatment, for example, and Jack is in remission according to his doctor. But there was no miraculous healing after the first prayer service where he came forward for help. And while the church is praying for Jack daily, ongoing therapy is still taking place. The remission is worthy of praise, but it's not the instant cure that the professional healer is offering at 2:00 Sunday afternoon.

The truth is that the professional healer's work will not be checked while he or she is in town. The healer can make a claim, declare the miracle to have happened, and by the time Jack learns whether or not the claims were accurate, the healer is long gone, and Jack may blame himself for a lapse in faith.

It is this ability to advertise a set time for miracles and then deliver the healings (or so it is claimed) that again separates the professional healer from the local clergy. Unless the minister is convinced that God always heals when asked, he or she is not going to try to deliver miracles on a schedule of human determination. The faith healer's advance publicity indicates that he or she does.

Second, most professional healers have staff who screen the people who come for healing. If you stand at the back of a professional healing service and observe what is taking place, you will notice how those with very obvious deformities are seldom given the instant cures pronounced for heart patients, cancer patients, and the like. Someone whose back is doubled forward from severe scoliosis, a person whose leg has been amputated at the knee, a person with a customized wheelchair to which he or she has been confined for many years, and others of a like nature will rarely be brought forward.

There are exceptions, of course. A few professional healers will instantly cure some who come forward and begin the process for others. Typical will be comments such as: "I can feel the healing power of the Lord surging into your back. God is beginning the healing process right now. You've been like this a long time, and you're not going to straighten instantly. Even God sometimes takes a few days for his miracles to become obvious. You can wait a few more days, can't you?" And invariably the person who is to be healed smiles or laughs with delight at the idea. Then the audience joins in, often with shouts of praise.

The healing is done in whatever manner the professional faith healer routinely uses. But instead of declaring the healing complete, which it obviously is not, the professional healer says, "I can see some changes already. It's just beginning, of course. Nothing dramatic. But if you ask me, you're standing a little straighter. Your back is a little stronger."

Then, turning to the audience, the professional healer may ask what they think. "Is the Lord working his miracles in this man today? Is the Lord's healing power in our midst?" And, of course, the healer's questions are answered with overwhelming shouts of agreement.

The professional healer counts on the fact that any act of contradiction may seem to reflect a lack of faith in God. Even if the person is doubtful that a miracle will occur, that any change is possible, there is a reluctance to admit to this. It's better to agree to the healer's pronouncements than risk the loss of that healing through the lack of faith.

Sometimes advance personnel will question those who wish to be healed. I have routinely witnessed this when the program is being televised, an observation shared by researchers such as MacArthur Foundation "genius grant" recipient James Randi, Professor Joseph Barnhart, professor of philosophy at North Texas University, a graduate of the

Southern Baptist Tehological Seminary, and others. Staff members will interview people, making notes about the person's name and problem, so that the professional healer can discuss it when talking briefly with the person before the healing. There is nothing dishonest about this. The cards are plainly visible. It is simply a time-saving method that can also be used to save embarrassment for the healer.

For example, in one service I witnessed a man who was deaf in one ear asked to be healed. The staff person went over to him and began talking quietly. "Are you expecting a miracle?"

"Well, I don't know. I hear some pretty good things about this fella, so I told my wife, if the doctors couldn't help me, maybe he could."

"There will be a doctor here today," said the staff person.

The man looked puzzled.

"Dr. Jesus. He's the one who really does the healings. Now I don't know about you, but I can feel the presence of Dr. Jesus right here in our midst. I've gone on a lot of these crusades, and I always feel his presence, his healing power. Why, I'll bet your ear feels a little stronger just being here."

The man smiled, then said, "I don't know about the ear, but the Spirit does seem to be moving here. Everybody's so friendly and all."

"You mean your ear doesn't seem like it's already beginning to heal just a bit, just being present here today? Not like you will hear after you're healed. Maybe just a little sound, like a whispering, not a mighty roar."

"Well, now that you mention it, the ear does seem different. Not that I can understand what you're saying unless I turn my good ear toward you. But maybe you're right. I just know I'm glad I came today."

"And you'll be even happier when God's healing takes place today."

There was nothing odd about the exchange. Two believers were seemingly sharing hope for the future. But as those who have studied professional faith healers have found, what the staff person was doing was determining whether or not the man could be used. If he were not healed by whatever methods were used, would he at least agree that healing was beginning? Would he, in other words, not spoil the show by saying, "You're a fraud. I'm still stone deaf."

Dr. Joseph Barnhart has studied faith healers and faith healings over the years. While many observers of faith healers proven to be frauds in at least a part of their actions feel that some of those "healed" are "ringers"—people brought in to fake being made well—Dr. Barnhart feels that there is far more involved.

During an interview with me Barnhart explained, "I think that the whole stage for these people [those seeking cures both for legitimate illness and other reasons] is the auditorium and the platform.... They make no great distinction. And this is in some ways a religio-magical drama in which they engage in sympathetic magic, that if they enact the scene, maybe this time the gods will come down and leave a miracle, so that it does not necessarily appear to them to be fraudulent."

Third, the whole healing service is like a scripted drama. Dr. Barnhart explained that the healers are like actors in a medieval morality play. "They are part of the great drama. I think if you press them, you can see the problems. In fact, I did press one of the older men and he got embarrassed." Dr. Barnhart discussed a man who participated in the healing service, though there was little wrong with him. He was old, retired, and his body was wearing out. He liked to walk each day to the fire station. Because of the affects of aging, however, he did have to stop on a bench part way to the fire station to catch his breath at times. There was no reason for him to be in the healing service in terms of his health, and he realized that when he was declared healed, nothing had happened to change his physical condition.

Dr. Barnhart explained one of his theories: The people who come for healing

> are people . . . who never get to shine or stand out. They may have wanted to be in the high school play, if they went to high school at all, and weren't.
>
> I noticed this one woman in particular, and she was just milking it for all it was worth. This was her moment of glory and grandeur, and she stole the scene from the preacher. She did what the preacher suggested, running back and forth, and praising God, and thanking Jesus. That sort of thing.
>
> It's somewhat scripted. It's a verbal ritual that's not deviated from too much.
>
> One of the things is that when the preacher asks you a question, you're supposed to give as positive an answer as you can because that's a reflection on God. Also, the positive answer is kind of an encouragement for God. It's sympathetic magic—act as if it is happening and maybe it will happen. In fact, I'm convinced that they believe that if they don't do that, they are lacking faith. . . . That's what faith is. It's going beyond the reality to enter into a new reality. Their frame of reference, at least for a time, is that it's this world, this empirical world we observe, that's the shadow. And the preacher can help catch you up into the real world of the spirit. It's inverted or reversed, and for a while, then, they can move into this new realm and actually believe that this healing is taking place.

Dr. Barnhart observed a situation in which the "players" in the drama did not act quite as anticipated. A woman came forward to be healed of a lump on her breast. The preacher declared her healed, then had her go into another room to examine herself. When she returned, she failed to respond as the preacher had hoped, her comments not pleasing him. Rather than continuing and risking embarrassment, he whirled around to the audience of many hundreds of people and declared that someone in the group had harbored thoughts of wanting to kill herself.

Now, in a large group of people in need of healing, the likelihood of finding a woman who has suicidal thoughts is fairly great. As a result, it was a safe area to approach, made safer still when a woman stood up, admitting that she had harbored such thoughts in the recent past. The preacher immediately turned away from the woman who had been "healed" of the breast tumor and focused on the new person, never returning to the former.

The willingness to go along with what was taking place became most obvious to Dr. Barnhart several years ago at a healing service of W. V. Grant, the son of a well-known faith healer by the same name. Professor Barnhart volunteered to be an usher after witnessing a number of elderly people sitting in wheelchairs well before the program and healing service were to begin. Wearing his large "usher" tag, Barnhart was better able to observe what was taking place backstage.

"I went over to the wheelchair people and I talked with them," he explained. "And I learned rather quickly that they did not come in those wheelchairs. That was all staged, prearranged." However he couldn't determine if advance arrangements had been made with local ministers for some of their elderly parishioners to come and be placed in wheelchairs or if the first elderly visitors to arrive at the service were simply placed in them. Whatever the case, a wheelchair was not their normal means for transportation.

> They were quite open with me. Since I was an usher, they thought I knew all of this anyhow.
>
> What I did, I just said that it must have been very difficult to get up the steps of this auditorium. The way they told me, they did not have any trouble except they were short of breath and it was hard climbing. And the way they

were explaining it all to me, they were talking about coming on foot. Those wheelchairs were not theirs.

Now after the service got started, he went out, of course, into the auditorium, in the aisles, and healed people who were blind and deaf, and various things, including one woman with a lump on her breast [the one mentioned earlier who was ignored after she refused to declare herself healed or to say there was a change in her condition]. It was standard procedure.

Then he went over to the people in the wheelchairs, and he interviewed them, talked with them, they did their dialogue together. The way he states the question was to give the audience the belief that they had been in those wheelchairs for years, and now they were going to be healed by Dr. Jesus. That was the way he put it.

So he got them out of the wheelchair and urged them to walk up the aisle—you've probably seen this on television—then run for Jesus. That sort of thing. And they would do a little shouting. And the crowd went absolutely wild.

It was all a part of the drama Dr. Barnhart described earlier. The audience members were gaining center stage for the first time in their lives. They knew nothing was wrong with them, but suddenly they were being treated with respect, with awe. They were important. All eyes were on them.

And part of the show is controlling what will happen. Kathryn Kuhlman was one of the masters at controlling her healing services. In print, she always stressed that it was Jesus who healed, not Kathryn Kuhlman.

> From the beginning, as now, I was wholly sure of two things: first, that I had nothing to do with what was happening, and second, I *knew* [emphasis hers] that it was the supernatural power of Almighty God. I have been satisfied to leave the why and the how to Him, for if I knew the answers to those two questions, then I would be God!

Or so she wrote in her book *I Believe in Miracles*. She continued:

In the light of God's great love, tenderness and compassion, the Holy Spirit revealed to me my worthlessness and helplessness of self. His greatness was overwhelming; I was only a sinner, saved by the Grace of God. The Power was His and the Glory, and this Glory, *His* [emphasis hers] Glory, He will not share with any human being.[8]

Still, the men and women who worked for Kuhlman in Pittsburgh claimed that she had enough of an ego that she delighted in letting others know that she was one of the chosen sinners through whom God healed. Yet such an ego does not come through in her writing.

Kuhlman, who also used the slaying-in-the-spirit technique, healed both by laying on of hands and by pronouncement ("I completely renounce that hernia in the balcony"). Though her staff frequently avoided allowing the severely handicapped to come forward, she was not afraid of failure. For example, a woman who had arthritis and was unable to bend over fully would be healed, then told to touch her toes. When she or others like her could not, Kuhlman would declare a partial healing to have been accomplished. Then the person would be told to return to her seat to pray for complete healing.

When writing about partial healings, Kathryn Kuhlman gave numerous specifics about those who could be interviewed by reporters at the time. She was the rare individual who did not try to "protect" the healed. Thus she discussed Bruce Baker's attendance at a healing service and his growing faith, while his complete healing took place in his home five days later.[9] And there was the story of Mary Schmidt who was freed from fear during a healing service, but then took months to achieve physical relief from goiter.[10]

It was unusual for Kuhlman to let someone who had been severely crippled come onto the stage except when that person could give testimony of past healing. A man who claimed to have been paralyzed from the waist down would walk onto the stage and show how he could now even dance. Someone with a previously paralyzed arm would show how strong it had become. The sighted would tell of past blindness. The formerly deaf would show they could hear. There were always at least two powerful men to assist anyone who came on stage, and her detractors claim that they would not let the obviously crippled come forward because the healings, if they occurred, were not likely to be the instant miracles the public wanted. Only if someone was so strong that he or she could move past them with relative ease would they step aside. Yet this could also have been an act of compassion since Kuhlman, in both instant and long-term healings, never predicted which would occur.

Were the healings legitimate? The believers never questioned, and Kuhlman always made certain that all glory went to God. The miracles, however, were frequently not witnessed during her broadcasts and public gatherings, a problem for contemporary researchers who prefer to confront the person and the person's doctor for corroboration. Fortunately for her supporters, Kuhlman did explain this, using real people when writing *I Believe in Miracles,* and her staff was known to collect medical documents when someone later came to her office to speak of their cures. Whether Kuhlman was as good as her supporters claim, or as bad as her detractors believe, she certainly was one of the more checkable of the faith healers.

The Unspoken Message

I'm disturbed by two unspoken messages that are sent in healing crusades handled by professional faith healers. The first is that the faith healer is special to God, that he or she has a better pipeline than the local minister. The second is that, just maybe, the faith healer is God's anointed—not on the level of Jesus, of course, but perhaps as close as a human can get.

Many professional faith healers add to their image and seeming legitimacy by having the local clergy sit on the stage as a part of the service. The local clergy become honored guests, though with several subtle implications. First is the reminder that the local clergy have never done what the visitor is doing. The local men and women are the nurturing, caring, competent clergy, but they are no miracle workers. And the visitor is a charismatic personality, confident, and healing instantly in God's name. Second, the local clergy on stage somehow legitimize the faith healer. The local clergy are trusted as people of God. Perhaps the local clergy can't work miracles, but their very presence on the stage is proof that the visiting faith healer can, indeed, fulfill the claims he or she makes.

Can we trust professional faith healers? Obviously that question can be answered only on a case-by-case basis. Some are frauds, dishonestly misleading people in order to gain financial benefits and ego satisfaction. Others are true believers who stress that it doesn't matter how many people they fail to heal; the glory is in the number of times they succeed. And most seem to fall somewhere in between, firmly believing in God, yet reaching people in a manner that occasionally requires their misrepresenting the truth a bit.

As I have said before, one of the key issues is accountability. No professional faith healer has ever provided substantial scientifically checkable proof of his or her claims for a broad range of cases. In many instances, the illnesses are self-proclaimed by the person to be healed, and the healing is praised based on the person's feelings. Some of the "healed" in this manner have come to feel themselves a part of a show. Others are living out a fantasy. Still others use the healer in place of needed medical care, later becoming sicker, often developing a chronic condition or dying.

But we must be careful not to confuse questionable practices by faith healers with the legitimacy of faith healing itself. The next two chapters will explore more fully the dynamics of fraudulent faith healers and the mysteries of healing, faith, and prayer.

3

The Fraudulent Healer

What can we learn to help us distinguish fraudulent healers from legitimate healers? A few examples from James Randi's book *Flim Flam* may clarify the issues a bit.[1]

DIAGNOSTICIANS

Randi cites the diagnosticians among the most common frauds. Diagnosticians are men and women who diagnose illness through one or another means other than surgery or standard medical procedures. This might mean psychic diagnosing through the reading of auras—the supposed color field of energy that surrounds the human body—or through some other approach. Some have a surprising success, though many medical professionals feel that it is likely such successful diagnosticians simply look for predictable and observable indicators in the human body. For example, someone with arthritis may have deformed joints. Certain heart conditions affect the eyes in ways someone can observe if they know what to look for. Discolored skin, odd body odors, and other obvious symptoms all can be spotted.

One diagnostician I interviewed took my hands, studied them, then diagnosed arthritis. Since my joints are deformed from a chronic, degenerative arthritic condition with which I have been troubled for the last twenty years, I was not impressed. Then, however, the woman mentioned that I had a serious problem with my lungs before my second birthday, a more impressive statement since I suffered from pneumonia at about eighteen months of age.

Was this diagnostician actually skilled? Perhaps. She already knew that lung problems had caused me to move to southern Arizona when I was in my twenties. At the time I spoke with her, well-publicized studies had been published of more than 4,000 British adults, starting with their births at the end of World War II. These studies tracked the medical aspects of their life development. The results, mentioned in the science sections of popular news magazines such as *Time* and *Newsweek,* revealed that early adult onset of any sort of lung problem usually occurred only in those people who had had a serious condition affecting their lungs before the age of two.

Typically diagnosticians rely on three different approaches to convince the public of their skills. The first is to stay within predictable limits. For example, if many older women are in the audience, it is safe for the diagnostician to call out diseases common to older women, like problems with reproductive organs. If many people in the audience are overweight, it is safe for the diagnostician to diagnose "sugar problems," which can mean anything from hypoglycemia (low blood sugar) to diabetes or high cholesterol. The diagnostician knows that if working-class people are in the audience, it is safe to say that several people will have either pains in their back or in their hands. Anyone who works on assembly lines or does repetitive work that is jarring in nature or involves weight lifting is likely to have arthritis or carpal tunnel syndrome. In addition, many people may have obvious joint damage from calcium buildup in the fingers. Some diagnosticians will hold the person's hands in order to unite them with God or whatever other reason they claim when they are actually doing nothing more than studying the joints for obvious signs of such diseases. Diagnosticians are skilled in checking a person's eyes, looking for scars, and checking a person's overall posture and appearance to make educated guesses. These guesses are so frequently correct that the diagnostician appears to have supernatural power.

The second approach diagnosticians use is to lead the person. "I see a problem with your back [chest or whatever]," is a common way to begin. If the person responds favorably, then the diagnostician will try to focus to whatever degree possible. For example, the person might react by unconsciously touching the upper or lower back, by touching the chest, or whatever is appropriate. This leads the diagnostician to the area of concern.

And the third approach, often used with the second, is to weave a fantasy, then get the person to agree with it. Because the people who seek such diagnosticians are eager either to get that person's approval or to be a part of the "show" during the healing ministry, he or she may go along with whatever the diagnostician says.

For example, James Randi studied Sue Wallace, a self-described doctor of magneto-therapy.[2] Once Wallace informed a woman that she had a problem with her right ovary. The woman explained that such a diagnosis was impossible since the ovary had been removed.

Wallace was insistent that there was no mistake. She

was quoted as saying, "Listen to me. These doctors take your money—you know?—and they do these operations, but they don't *need* to—you know?—and just because they cut out your ovary, I mean, the trouble is still there. I'm getting it . . ."[3]

Wallace eventually stated that the problem was in the *area* of the right ovary. When the woman argued, Wallace "fixed the patient with a glare and asked, 'But you've had headaches, haven't you?' The answer, not unsurprisingly, was yes. 'That's the first sign,' said Miss Wallace ominously. 'You'll see.'"[4]

The one point that must be said in favor of Sue Wallace is that she is apparently quite sincere. Unlike some diagnosticians, she agreed to be tested by Randi, who agreed to pay her $10,000 if she passed a scientifically sound, double-blind test. She had a large sum of money to win, her credibility to lose, at least among those who read about the test. Although she was unable to pass Randi's test, she did exhibit conviction and belief in her own abilities, and she met a challenge many other diagnosticians have avoided.

Unfortunately, many faith healers are not concerned with scientific testing or any other proof. They want to show that they can call on God to create a miracle, right here, right now! And often they will use the same trickery that professional magicians and con artists use, playing off their followers' faith, naïveté, or gullibility.

W. V. GRANT

For example, in 1986 CBS television explored Walter Vinson (W. V.) Grant on its short-lived news program "West 57th Street." Grant, a Dallas-based healer in his early forties at the time, is the son of a former tent preacher who was a firm believer that Satan lived on the moon with his devils, that UFOs were real, and that there was a constant warfare with demons.[5]

Young W. V. Grant was far more mainstream than his father. He learned from his father that direct mail can be profitable, but he saw a better approach than the one his father had used. The older man had produced religious pamphlets that were extremist enough to be the object of ridicule from mainstream Christians, yet they sold in such large numbers that he became quite wealthy. The son produced different, less extreme mail-order products, which earned his work greater acceptability. For example, he offered a Bible course by mail. This was a familiar type of program offered by many denominations for Christians seeking to expand their knowledge through home study. However, where most mainstream groups considered such courses to be continuing education, providing nothing more than a certificate of completion, W. V. Grant sold the course as a vehicle for changing careers. When the course was completed, the person received a diploma listing him or her as "reverend." An honorary doctorate also accompanied the diploma, along with a license to preach.[6] Only the license to preach had any real value for the recipient because some states and cities will license people to perform weddings and similar rites if they can show they represent a religious group. The license to preach, although meaningless compared to the credentials of someone receiving an in-depth education, still meets legal requirements to obtain all the tax advantages and other clergy perquisites if the person starts his or her own church.

Grant called attention to himself through the media because he had a tendency to exaggerate his education and his abilities. He claimed to be a high school football hero, but the record he claimed was disputed by the former coach and did not show up in the school records. In addition, one of the degrees on his wall at the time of the CBS study was from Midstates Bible College in Des Moines, Iowa. The trouble was, either the school did not exist in 1972, or it lacked accreditation and even a telephone.

Other claims concerning the success of his television program and the scope of his ministry also proved to be exaggerated. Faith healing was the mainstay of his work, and some of his followers expressed relief for extraordinary healings—a reversed hysterectomy, for example.

In the mid-1980s, Grant liked to heal people in wheelchairs. The healed person would jump out of the chair, often doing a little dance, then would wheel the chair down the aisle after the healing. Interviews with people who were "healed," however, often revealed that they had a medically diagnosed disease such as cancer, though not so severe that they couldn't walk. When the ill people arrived at the healing service, they were placed in a wheelchair, no one ever saying their illness prevented them from walking. The wheelchair, however, implied it.[7]

One tip-off that the professional faith healer is practicing a scam comes when a person truly unable to walk, riding on a customized wheelchair, enters the healing service. Either the person is ignored, prayed for, or told that the healing is "beginning to work." After all, the infirmity took months or years to develop to its present extreme, the professional healer will explain. If God chooses to take a few days to complete his miracle, that is understandable. Thus the person may look the same on the outside, may not be leaving the chair, but the healing miracle is taking place. This type of "healing" was frequently used by Grant when he risked working with someone truly unable to walk.

The other trick used by Grant and others was to help the blind to see. Sometimes this was the result of a simple misrepresentation of facts. For example, my wife is legally blind—without her glasses. Normally she wears contact lenses or extremely thick lenses on her eyeglasses, and with these intense visual aids, she is able to read, drive a car, and perform as a professional singer and actress. But take away her glasses, and she must have an object within inches of her face to be certain what it is.

Grant and others used people like my wife for their healing services. The people would acknowledge that they were blind, which in fact they were. Then the "healing" would take place, and the healer would hold fingers in front of the blind people's face or have them read the Bible (deliberately held close to their eyes). When the "blind" man or woman read the Bible, the audience applauded, another miracle was declared, and no one mentioned the degrees of legal blindness.

When James Randi investigated W. V. Grant, he found another trick. According to Randi, Grant used a directional microphone, which picked up voices in a very limited area. If Grant pointed the microphone toward his subject, then spoke, the microphone would record only the voice of the subject. By contrast, if Grant pointed it toward his own mouth and the subject spoke, the microphone would not record the subject. At times Grant would tell a man he was healed of his blindness, hold up a number of fingers, and ask the man to tell him how many fingers he was holding up. Then, as Grant pointed the microphone toward the man, Grant would say the number loud enough for the man to hear him. Because of the narrow directional nature of the microphone, however, the television cameras (which were fed sound by the directional mike) wouldn't pick up the healer's voice. They would record only the voice of the "healed" man, who repeated the number, implying he could see. And another miracle would be declared.[8]

Oddly, over the years, many newspapers, including the *Dallas Morning News,* Grant's hometown paper, revealed his tricks. But either the followers didn't read the reports or they chose not to believe them, a common situation with faith healers.

WHAT MAKES HEALERS RESORT TO FRAUD?

What makes faith healers—people ostensibly devoted to revealing the power of God to heal—resort to fraudulent practices? What causes people who start out having faith in God's healing power end up believing in their own power to heal? What causes people whose goal is to heal people to *use* them instead?

The reasons are many and complex. But perhaps at the top of the list are ego needs, greed, the need for success, and the need to have God be "successful."

Ego Needs

As we noted before, people involved in faith healing receive wide recognition and acclaim. For some people, this recognition is addictive. They need the ego boost, the high that comes from being the center of attention, from having power, from having people need them.

Their need to be in control, their need to be godlike drives them beyond the boundaries of legitimacy. They forget that healing power comes from God, and they begin to believe in their own power. They begin to believe their own tricks.

Greed

In 1858, Bernadette Soubrious, an uneducated peasant girl in Lourdes, France, claimed to have been visited by Mary, the mother of Jesus, whom she called "the lady." Within two decades, the town took advantage of this miracle visitation to create an impressive industry.[9] A visit that may or may not have happened, for reasons that may or may not have had anything to do with healing, resulted in what people consider the faith-healing center of the world.

Today Lourdes survives on tourism, with five million visitors coming each year. Considering the money these visitors pay to the approximately 400 hotels, the food they consume in the restaurants, and the religious souvenirs they purchase, Lourdes is perhaps the wealthiest city in the world to be supported primarily on human suffering.

Everything about Lourdes becomes sacred to the hucksters. Tiny containers of the Lourdes' grotto's spring water is sold to the tourists, and even more of the water is consumed for either drinking or ritual washing. The bottlers, sellers, and faithful partakers claim that this water has curative powers. The Catholic Church, however, has never officially claimed that the water was anything more than a rather foul smelling mineral water no different from any other water to be found in other parts of France. If it is unique in some way, it is probably because it is rather contaminated from all the bodies using it.

Merchants sell religious statues, booklets, and anything else they can convince the tourists to buy. Some of the merchants are "crazies" who find the desperate visitors ideal targets for what they have to market. Others are shrewd business people who know how to exploit emotional desperation in the same manner that Las Vegas, Reno, Atlantic City, and Monaco have been exploiting economic desperation. And the carefully choreographed candle-lit processions that make for such moving and dramatic photographs are no different from the opulent interiors of the casinos. They are flash and show, signifying nothing according to the Catholic Church.

Why so cynical about a place of spiritual healing? Perhaps because even the Catholic Church is cynical about Lourdes. The stories of the miracles are often repeated by priests and nuns, telling of the glory of God. Yet in more than a century of "miracles," even the Catholic Church has declared only approximately one hundred of the claims so well documented as to be believable. And fewer than three-fourths of these documented claims have been declared "miracles" within the belief system of the church's hierarchy.

Other healers driven by greed include some televangelists who use the uncheckable to support their bank accounts. I took a break from writing this book to watch a well-established television minister. He was in the midst of healing people in his audience. Or perhaps I should say that God was healing some of the people, and the evangelist was just providing the play-by-play for the audience. God was the quarterback, and the televangelist was the sports reporter, telling the crowd of another gridiron miracle.

The televangelist told of someone (presumably but not necessarily in the viewing audience) who had trouble with his or her leg. The healing was not gender specific, though it can be assumed that God knew the difference. The televangelist began stroking his own knee to show that the pain was in the joints. He told of how the sufferer sometimes awakens with discomfort in the middle of the night. He told that the person has to work the leg in ways that make it feel better when the sufferer awakens in the morning.

But God was in the process of healing that leg "right now." This was not an instant cure, of course. It would take time. But, praise the Lord, the miracle healing was going on while the televangelist was speaking.

Many facts were left unreported to the audience, of course, not the least of which was why God would mention to the televangelist all details except the name of the person he was healing. There always are omissions in such long-distance miracle reports.

I have a hard time taking such "healings" seriously.

First, knee discomfort is one of the most common problems people have. People who jog are at risk for knee damage. Potassium deficiency as well as arthritis and osteoporosis can cause problems with the knees. Certainly there were within the audience, both in the studio and in the television audience, many people who could relate to the discomfort described by the televangelist.

The evangelist declared several other healings God was doing, always using examples that would be familiar to people. Then he explained how God's work could continue only if the viewers would send money to support the televangelist's ministry.

The implication was clear. God was healing, yet somehow, without the televangelist providing the play-by-play of what God was doing, he might stop. Or perhaps God would become angry. Or . . .

Whatever the case, the ministry was related to the miracle of those healings, and the ministry had to be preserved at all costs. After all, there was no telling what God might or might not do if those checks didn't keep coming in to pay for the television time.

At no time did the televangelist suggest that viewers might have better use for their time and money, such as volunteering at a hospital or hospice, attending a church, and visiting the shut-ins. The evangelist made no effort to move viewers into their communities, where they could be involved in social interaction and direct caring and sharing. Viewers were to stay in isolation in whatever room the television was located. They were to send in money so God's healings could continue. And they were to rejoice with the people on the television set, not with those in "real life" who would relish a visitor, a kind word, a reason to continue to have the will to live.

The Need to Be Successful

Faith healers often turn to fraudulent practices because they have a strong need to be successful. If the people who come to them aren't healed, their credibility will wane, and people will stop coming. This need for success drives them to exaggeration, false claims, and tricks. If the people who come to the faith healers never challenge the healers' claims, the healers gain courage to continue the deception. Soon fraud becomes the norm for these healers.

The process from a few minor deceptions to major fraud may happen over an extended period of time. The healer may never have intended to use fraudulent practices, but power is seductive. The attention of the crowd, as we said before, is addictive. And to maintain that attention, the healer must continue to be successful.

Those whose actions and attitudes are questionable at best, fraudulent at worst, must convince their followers that their healings work. Since they know that this will not always be the case, they try to work around the issue. First, they create an environment where the person coming to them will claim to be healed, even if he or she senses no change. In fact, the psychology of the healing service, from the intense use of music to set a joyous mood of celebration and praise at the beginning, to the peer pressure to claim a victory over pain and illness, prevent many people from telling the truth. And in some cases, the people may not even know the truth, their emotions masking the signs of whatever afflicts them.

In other instances, the person for whom a healing is proclaimed recognizes that nothing has happened. The breast lump does not wither. The deformed leg is not miraculously straightened and healed. The man with the severed spinal cord does not rise from his wheelchair and walk.

To avoid the deep disappointment and occasional anger

directed at them, fraudulent healers often resort to blaming the ill person for lack of sufficient faith needed to be healed. "Place your faith wholeheartedly in God. Don't waver, don't doubt. If you doubt, the healing will not take place," they chant.

Or healers remain "successful" by convincing ill people that a healing has started. The wheelchair-bound person doesn't rise and walk because the healing will take some time. Instead, healers use suggestions to get people to say they feel a slight tingling sensation in the previously useless legs or maybe some warmth that wasn't there before. Whatever idea the person agrees to results in prayerful praise and a declaration of success. "You'll be dancing at my next crusade, praise the Lord!" the healer may say, and the smiling, still-disabled person is wheeled from the stage, grateful for whatever may be happening.

The Need to Have God Succeed

Sometimes faith healers turn to deception because they can't live with the mysteries of healing; they need to have God be "successful." As we will discuss in the next chapter, healing is a mystery. How God heals, whom he heals, when he heals is beyond human understanding. But some healers are unable to accept a God who heals one person but not another, who heals in a variety of ways.

In their inability to accept God for who he is, some faith healers feel they need to give God help. If God doesn't heal a certain person, these healers want to save God the embarrassment. They can't live with the possibility that God may have chosen not to heal a particular person on a particular day in a particular way. So they fudge a little, making it look as if the person is healed rather than have God come off looking "unsuccessful."

In their inability to live with open-endedness, these healers force the issue through deception and fraud. What is sad about this dynamic is that in trying to "protect" God, these fraudulent healers do more to damage God's name than they realize. These fraudulent healers have given a bad name not only to God but also to the genuine healers and to the whole issue of faith healing.

For any number of reasons, some faith healers are frauds. We do ourselves, other people, and the healers themselves a favor by using discernment. We must be aware of certain actions that suggest deception and fraud. We must be alert to situations that lend themselves to fraud. And we must be ready to challenge the claims of healers whom we suspect of fraud.

Genuine faith healers will not be afraid to admit that God doesn't always heal people. Genuine faith healers will not be threatened by follow-up procedures. Genuine faith healers will be quick to divert people's attention from themselves, the healers, to a holy, sovereign God, the master Healer.

4

Healing, Faith, and Prayer

Healing of *any* kind is a mystery. Who can begin to understand the intricacies of the immune system as it combats disease? Who can explain why the same treatment will cure one person but not another? Who can explain how some people will get well while others either stay the same or get worse? Who can explain how doctors can heal one person but not another person with the same condition? Who can explain how prayer heals some diseases that doctors and medicine have not been able to heal?

Who can solve this dilemma? People have come to outright frauds and the ill person's faith has made them well. And people have come to devout, sincere healers trying to share their understanding of God, to claim no power or glory for themselves, and the sick have remained as sick as they were before the laying on of hands, prayer, or similar action. It is a reality that defies human logic.

Such experiences are not much different from those in contemporary medicine. A percentage of patients seeing a physician will get well no matter what the doctor chooses to do or not to do for treatment. And a percentage of patients will not recover, regardless of medicine, surgery, change of diet, or any other action.

For the vast majority of people, healing seems to be a combination of factors including rest, loving care, prayer, perhaps surgery, medication, a change of diet, or a change of exercise. Healing is a mystery.

Understanding healing becomes even more complex when we realize that in some situations the "good" people die from illness and the "wicked" get well. During the early experiments with artificial hearts, the most successful patient, the person who lived the longest with the fewest complications, was a Swedish man who had been involved with organized crime. Sometimes the whole thing doesn't seem fair.

In his autobiography, J. B. Phillips, paraphraser of *The New Testament in Modern English,* expresses similar puzzlement at how God works to heal people. He had in his parish a woman who had deep spiritual insight and also possessed the "gift of healing":

> She was very reticent about this and would normally only lay hands on anyone who was sick if she strongly felt it was God's will for her to do so.
>
> I well remember being present when Olive laid her hands upon a middle-aged man with an inoperable cancer. Within a week I saw with my own eyes that the growth had disappeared, and the doctors soon pronounced him fit. He lived for another twenty years after that. This man was a good husband and father, but I would not say that he was a man of especially robust faith. At the same time of his particularly malignant disease there lay another man, this time one of strong and active faith, in terrible pain through cancer of some part of the spine. I used to visit him, pray

with him and generally try to keep up his courage. Finally, I decided to persuade Olive to lay hands on him. Surely what God had accomplished with one sufferer He could do for another. Olive took a lot of persuasion but she did finally lay hands on the tormented man with spinal cancer. Faith was certainly present, but nothing even by way of temporary relief was granted, and in another two weeks, the sufferer was dead.

Despite my ensuing bewilderment (which continues to this day) I was myself persuaded to lay hands on those who asked for it in a brief service which followed the Wednesday morning celebration of holy communion. I have no gift of healing myself . . . and I did this as Christ's representative, possibly as an ordained man I might be a channel of his healing power. Nothing dramatic happened, but I do know of several people who felt their tensions relax and their normal attitude to life change from one of fear to one of faith, which is in itself a kind of miracle. And I also remember one old lady, who was constantly in terrible pain, telling me in a wholly uncharacteristically sweet voice that she "had no more pain." A few weeks later she died peacefully and serenely with no recurrences of her agonies.

I have no doubts at all that God *does* heal people through the agency of certain gifted persons, but I am still more than a little puzzled by the apparently sporadic distribution of the gift, and the apparently capricious way of its working. I have also become convinced that a good deal of nonsense is spoken and written about healing. There are meetings where fit youngish healers have by sheer force of personality persuaded trembling old ladies that they were healed. (Of course if they relapsed afterward it was because of their own lack of faith.) By all means let the subject be studied without prejudice but let the healers practice with scrupulous honesty as well as with compassion.[1]

These kinds of situations have led people like Sandy (not her real name) to ask if illness is related to sin and healing to right living. In Sandy's early adult life she lived what she considered a rather sinful life. She had been having sex out of wedlock, drinking more than she should, and occasionally using marijuana.

Several years later Sandy decided to quit her destructive lifestyle. She sought God's help through prayer and the reading of Scripture. For several months she abstained from all alcohol and drugs. She returned to church and was actively involved with the young adult programs. She found a young man she wanted to marry, and despite her promiscuous past, she realized she should wait for sexual fulfillment until she was married. She also found a good job, worked hard, and acted responsibly.

Then Sandy's world collapsed when a routine medical exam revealed a large malignant mass in her brain stem. Because the mass was intertwined with the delicate parts of her brain stem, the mass couldn't be removed surgically. Specialists ruled out radiation and chemotherapy as treatment options.

"So where was God?" she cried out to her priest. She was angry, deeply hurt, not certain if she wanted to weep or curse God. "Had this happened while I was living wildly, I would have understood. My actions would have deserved this as punishment. But Father Joe, I was doing everything right. God's not supposed to let things like that happen to us when we're doing everything right, is he?"

The priest added, "How do you explain God's mystery, his wisdom, his love to someone who's going through such an ordeal? There's nothing in the Bible that says God rewards all good and punishes all evil. Good people suffer from time to time, and bad people have occasionally prospered on this earth. Even the good can have bad in them, like King David, who sent his girlfriend's husband to the front line to be killed so he could marry her. If ever there was God's beloved, it was David, an adulterer as well as the possible creator of so many of those beautiful psalms of praise."[2]

It is not the purpose of this book to answer the questions of *why* God does certain things, but situations like Sandy's point out the complexities of our understanding of the interrelationship of illness and healing, faith and sin, prayer and God's power.

THE ROLE OF FAITH IN HEALING

How does a person's faith in God affect his or her ability to be healed? Does God somehow measure a person's faith and then determine whether or not he will heal that person based on the quantity or quality of that faith? Does he look at the young man suffering from lupus and say, "Well, Don's faith isn't quite strong enough yet. I'll wait to heal him until it grows a bit more"? What part does faith play?

When we look at the Gospels' accounts of Christ healing people, we notice several dynamics. First, Christ *acknowledged* the faith of people who came to him. Of the centurion, who knew that if Jesus just spoke the word his servant would be healed, Christ said, "I have not found such great faith even in Israel" (Luke 7:9).

Second, Christ *points out the interrelationship of faith and healing*. To the woman who was healed when she touched his cloak, he said, "Daughter, your faith has healed you" (Luke 8:48). To the blind beggar who asked Jesus to give him his sight, Jesus said, "Receive your sight; your faith has healed you" (Luke 18:42). We must be careful here not to jump to an illogical conclusion: that if these people had not had faith, Christ would not have healed them.[3]

Third, Christ *challenges* people's faith, wanting it to grow. In Luke's account of the story of Jairus, a synagogue ruler who comes to ask Jesus to heal his dying daughter, Jesus is on the way to Jairus' house when he is delayed by the woman who touched his cloak and was healed of a twelve-year hemorrhage. During this delay, Jairus' servant comes to tell him that he need not bother Jesus anymore because his daughter has died. Hearing the servant's words, Jesus turns to Jairus and says, "Don't be afraid; just believe, and she will be healed" (Luke 8:50).

Fourth, Christ points out a *lack of faith* in some situations. When the disciples were unable to heal a boy from destructive seizures, Christ steps in and heals the boy. Puzzled, the disciples ask Jesus why they weren't able to do it. Christ's reply is, "Because you have so little faith" (Matt. 17:20). In another passage, Matthew comments on Christ's visit to his hometown: "And he did not do many miracles there because of their lack of faith" (Matt. 13:58).

Fifth, Christ's goal is to *increase people's faith in God*. After Christ heals a man ravaged by demons, he tells the man, "Return home and tell how much God has done for you" (Luke 8:39).

POSITIVE ROLE OF FAITH IN HEALING

What we can say from looking at these Gospel accounts is that faith enables healing. The passages suggest that Christ heals in response to a person's faith.

But we must be quick to point out that faith is not necessarily a requirement for healing. In the Old Testament story of Naaman, discussed in chapter 2, Naaman doesn't necessarily have faith that bathing seven times in the Jordan River will cure his leprosy. In fact he vigorously resists the idea in the beginning. When he finally complies, he does so out of obedience. And to his surprise, his leprosy disappears. He returns to Elisha, exclaiming, "Now I know that there is no God in all the world except in Israel" (2 Kings 5:15). Faith, in this story is the *result* of the healing, not the *requirement*.

It's also important to recognize the *object* of the faith:

the faith is in God's power, not in the healer or in the method. After Naaman is healed, he doesn't come back to Elisha saying, "Boy, that's some river you've got here. That water is powerful stuff!" Similarly, Elisha doesn't hang out a shingle announcing that he is a healer. He doesn't bottle Jordan River water and sell it to everyone who has leprosy. Elisha recognizes that the sovereign God chose to heal a particular man in a particular way for a particular purpose: so that he would know the true God.

The New Testament echoes this dynamic. When in the middle of a crowd a woman was healed by touching Christ's cloak, the people didn't conclude that Christ's cloak had special powers, that if only they could tear off pieces of his cloak, they would have a permanent source of healing. Christ's words to the woman indicate that it was her faith in God, not her faith in some magic powers inherent in his clothing, that he recognized.

This has implications for contemporary healing and healers. When healers ask people to put their faith in a certain person, object, or method, they are asking for faith in the wrong thing. It is God who heals, not the magic touch from a healer. It is God who heals, not the water from a certain spring. It is God who heals, not the money given to a certain healing ministry.

MANIPULATIVE ROLE OF FAITH IN HEALING

Faith can also be used in manipulative ways in healing services. This is what we have seen in previous chapters to be true of some fraudulent faith healers. These healers try to conjure up faith. Music, shouts of praise, and cameras are used to bring the electricity of the "Spirit" into the meeting. Please don't misunderstand me. Music and praise are not bad. But when they are used by faith healers to force an atmosphere that whips up faith, then they are false.

A second type of manipulation occurs when faith healers talk about the faith needed to be healed. The healer makes it clear that healing is a partnership. God can and will work miracles, but only in those with sufficient faith to receive them. The implication is that anyone who is not healed during the service has not attained adequate faith. They are not yet right with God. There will be a second chance, of course, and a third, and a fourth. The healing becomes a proficiency test. The person who needs healing can work on his or her faith, trying to strengthen it to the minimum standard God demands. Although the theological basis for such an attitude is unsound, the fraudulent healer uses it to explain a situation in which a person is not healed. The healer manipulates faith for his or her own benefit. The healer blames the ill person for not having enough faith.

THE ROLE OF PRAYER IN HEALING

What role does prayer play in the healing process? People see three options here: prayer has no place in healing; prayer is the only way people are healed; and God heals through a combination of prayer and other means.

For most non-Christians, prayer has no place in the healing process. For them, healing comes through scientific, medical procedures, through the work of medical professionals and modern technology. When they get sick, they go to a doctor, take the prescribed medication, and never think to pray to God about their condition. It is interesting to observe, however, that often non-Christians who become seriously ill will ask a relative or hospital chaplain for prayer. Even though the ill people have no active faith practice, their instincts are to reach out to God when they are sick.

Some religious groups believe prayer is the only way people are healed. These groups do not allow the intervention of medical science or technology. In chapter 7, I will discuss the Church of Christ, Scientist, which severely limits the involvement of medical intervention for its members.

Christians who are in the field of health care frequently say that prayer is critical for health. Many are involved in groups that actively use prayer, including the laying on of hands, for healing. Yet they also feel that medical skills, pharmaceuticals, and surgical techniques are also among God's gifts. They see them as blessings to be used in healing those who are suffering. Using medicine—whether an aspirin or a quadruple bypass surgery—all the time recognizing that the skills and the knowledge come from God, seems well within line of what Jesus wanted. They believe that God can and sometimes does heal without medical intervention but that he often chooses to use modern medical techniques.

Several interesting studies have attempted to document the power of prayer on the healing process. In July of 1988, the *Southern Medical Journal,* the publication of the Alabama-based Southern Medical Association, published a paper by Randolph C. Byrd, M.D., of San Francisco. The article, entitled "Positive Therapeutic Effects of Intercessory Prayer in a Coronary Care Unit Population," reported on a ten-month study of 393 patients in the coronary care unit.

The patients were chosen for the similarity of their coronary (heart) problems. They were randomly divided into two groups: one group of 192 patients had Christians outside the hospital pray for them; the other group of 201 patients (the control group) had no group praying for them. None of the patients knew in which group they had been placed.

Dr. Byrd and his staff were not allowed to know which patients were being prayed for and which were not. The original selection was made at random by the computer.

Then the intercessors were chosen according to the following criteria:

> They were "born again" Christians with an active Christian life as manifested by daily devotional prayer and active Christian membership with a local church. Members of several Protestant churches and the Roman Catholic Church were represented among the intercessors. Patients and intercessors were not matched by religion or denomination. After randomization, each patient was assigned to three to seven intercessors. The patients' first name, diagnosis, and general condition were given to the intercessors. The intercessory prayer was done outside of the hospital daily until the patient was discharged from the hospital. Under the direction of a coordinator, each intercessor was asked to pray daily for a rapid recovery and for prevention of complications and death, in addition to other areas of prayer they believed to be beneficial to the patient.

The end results of the study were significant. The patients for whom intercessory prayers were made recovered faster and had a greatly reduced need for antibiotics, diuretics, and intubation/ventilation. Their time in the hospital was less traumatic, and they had fewer complications.[4]

There have been other studies along these lines, such as one in 1965 reported in the *Journal of Chronic Disease* and one in 1969, reported in *Medical Times*. The former study involved rheumatic patients; the latter involved leukemic children. Both studies were far smaller—thirty-eight patients in the first, and eighteen children in the second—and those results, though weighted toward the value of prayer, were too limited to be conclusive. There seemed to be no question, however, that the study done in San Francisco was strong enough so that the value of prayer, in combination with consistent medical treatment, cannot be denied.

Why People Go to Faith Healers

What makes people seek out healing through faith and prayer? Some people go to faith healers because they strongly believe in the power of God to heal through men and women to whom he gives healing gifts. They have seen evidence of these healings—perhaps a friend's brain tumor disappeared after healing prayer, or a relative has been healed from emotional illness through prayer offered by intercessors in his church—and they want to be part of the flow of God's power.

For other people the faith healer represents the only chance they may have for recovery. Sometimes the people who attend such a healing session have truly exhausted all hope. They may have gone the route of not only traditional medicine but also nontraditional approaches, ranging from radical diet changes to experimental drugs and surgeries.

Others rely on faith healers because they are the only "doctors" they can afford. A large segment of American society lacks health insurance and access to traditional medical care. Another portion comes from a background where health care was traditionally so poor, the only reason they went to a doctor was to have their teeth pulled when they rotted, to have a bone set when it was broken, and to be cared for while they died.

Still other people believe they need an intermediary to pray to God. These are people who have frequently spent their lives feeling demeaned. They believe strongly in God, but they do not feel worthy of a direct blessing. They need an intermediary, someone better than themselves, to gain God's miraculous healing power.

Whatever the reason, hundreds of people go to faith healers. If these healers are frauds, they can do more harm than good by abusing God-given gifts and by abusing God's name.

5

Illness and Demonic Influence

One of the more controversial aspects of understanding the relationship of faith and healing is the whole issue of illness and demonic influence. Over the centuries, various cultures have linked illness to the influence of demons. Sometimes that link is superficial, as in a typical response to a sneeze, "God bless you." The more accurate response, according to the superstition, is "God bless you, the devil miss you." This response is rooted in the now-forgotten belief that when you sneeze, goodness has been expelled, leaving an empty space. Unless God protects and blesses you, the devil will use that brief opening to enter your body.

Other times the link between illness and demons is more direct. The idea that demons existed as causes of human suffering was an ancient one that predated Judaism and the Old Testament writings. Primitive peoples believed that evil spirits caused all major forms of suffering and evil, including disease.

Each culture that practiced one or another of the pagan religions had teachings about such demons, and their ideas were quite familiar to the men and women of the Old Testament times. Some of the early Hebrews felt that God created demons before the world was made. Others felt that demons were the offspring of angels who turned against God, came to earth, and married the beautiful daughters of the early men. It was even believed that some of the demons staked out territory from which they could be dangerous to humans, such as the demon Azazel, who was thought to live in the wilderness, attacking pilgrims who chanced his way.[1]

The Greeks believed that a demon was a little like a contemporary ghost, and the most dangerous demons to the Greeks were the spirits of the unburied dead. They caused natural disasters and sickness, but they could be controlled through various rituals like magic, incantations, and the like.

The people in these early cultures did not understand illness—biology, the immune system, bacteria, and viruses. Instead, they found it easy to explain life's problems by ascribing these mysteries to the activities of evil demons. They would say that demons cause a good person to die from dehydration following a severe illness in which he was having uncontrollable diarrhea and vomiting.

Some cultures believed demons to be malevolent mischief makers, somewhat vicious practical jokers. Others seduce humans away from performing acts of goodness.[2] Still others can take possession of someone, turning them into an out-of-control robot of evil.[3] And still others have been seen as the mortal enemies of humans, determined to do what is necessary to destroy their physical bodies and souls.[4]

These beliefs of ancient cultures about evil spirits

prevented them from learning anatomy and physiology. Some people feared corpses, believing that the dead spread death. Others felt that spirits of the dead would cause danger to the healthy who came too close to them. And some felt that to defile a corpse in any way, including by studying the body, was an act against God. Whatever the belief, though, methods used to understand anatomy, physiology, traumatic injury, disease, and death that are common today were considered sacrilegious at best and potentially deadly at worst during the time preceding and during the Old and New Testaments. Thus there was no way to learn if there were alternative ways to consider illness, injury, and death. Demon possession and similar causes were both logical and could not be countered by other knowledge because there was no other knowledge acceptable to the majority of the people at the time.

A NEW TESTAMENT PERSPECTIVE

The New Testament also suggests a relationship between healing and demons.[5] It's interesting to note that the emphasis on demons and demon possession is a phenomenon found in only the gospels of Matthew, Mark, and Luke; John didn't emphasize such stories.

Although the relationship between healing and demonic activity is a complex one that deserves more careful examination than this chapter will give it, let's look at some broad suggestions made by the gospel writers. I see at least three categories emerging: illness is not always related to demons; illness is sometimes related to demons; and illness is sometimes *caused* by demons. Let's examine each of the suggested beliefs a bit more closely.

Illness isn't always related to demons. In chapter 2 we reviewed the variety of Christ's healing miracles Luke reports in his gospel. Many of these illnesses were not at all related to demon involvement. Peter's mother-in-law, the untouchable leper, the centurion's servant, the woman's hemorrhage, a crippled woman, the blind beggar, and others were healed, and in each case Luke made no mention of demon involvement in the illness.

Illness is sometimes related to demons. In several of the healing miracles recorded in the New Testament, the Gospels seem to suggest that healing and casting out of demons went hand-in-hand. The verses do not suggest a causal relationship, but they indicate that healing illness and casting out demons were two parts of a larger whole— bringing a person to spiritual, physical, and mental wholeness.

For instance, a passage in Matthew says, "When evening came, many who were demon-possessed were brought to [Jesus], and he drove out the spirits with a word and healed all the sick" (Matt. 8:16). In a similar passage "The people brought to Jesus all the sick and demon-possessed. The whole town gathered at the door, and Jesus healed many who had various diseases. He also drove out many demons. . . ." (Mark 1:32–34). News of Christ's ministry "spread all over Syria, and people brought to him all who were ill with various diseases, those suffering severe pain, the demon possessed, those having seizures, and the paralyzed, and he healed them" (Matt. 4:24).

When Christ chose his twelve disciples, "He gave them power and authority to drive out all demons and to cure diseases, and he sent them out to preach the kingdom of God and to heal the sick" (Luke 9:1). "[The disciples] went out and preached that people should repent. They drove out many demons and anointed many sick people with oil and healed them" (Mark 6:13).

Illness is sometimes caused *by demons.* Still other passages suggest that some illnesses Jesus and his disciples healed were cured through the casting out of a demon or demons.

For instance, Matthew records a story in which, ". . . a man who was possessed and could not talk was brought to Jesus. And when the demon was driven out, the man who had been mute spoke" (Matt. 9:32–34). This suggests a more direct relationship; the demons seem to be causing the man's inability to speak. Or in a similar passage, the people "brought [Jesus] a demon-possessed man who was blind and mute, and Jesus healed him, so that he could talk and see " (Matt. 12:22). In a third incident, Matthew tells that a boy who had seizures was brought to Jesus. "Jesus rebuked the demon, and it came out of the boy, and he was healed from that moment" (Matt. 17:14–18).

Exorcisms were not new to the time of Jesus. What was different with his ministry was his statement that he was using the power of God to exorcise. By the end of New Testament times, biblical scholars and religious seekers were left with often conflicting ideas about health and healing. Some concepts were rejected; others were embraced. And the search for healing and the roles of God and humans in combating emotional, physical, and spiritual illness had become more complex than ever.

MISUNDERSTANDING ABOUT DEMON POSSESSION

Demon possessions of one sort or another were reported in ancient times. Often they were used to explain the unexplainable, such as physical and mental illness. At other times, demon possession was the answer to unwanted traits.

For example, some people believed that when an infant cried more than the parents saw fit, it was either a demon in human form or a human possessed by the devil. Beatings were regularly administered, and the infant might be killed when "necessary" in extreme circumstances.[6]

Some European families felt that their infant became possessed by being curious and exploring his or her surroundings. And the mark of that possession, the proof that the demon was in them, came when the child turned into an "animal" by crawling on the floor. The parents did not understand that a child will almost always crawl before he or she learns to walk.[7]

Abuses

Because of a lack of understanding of the role of demons in illness, some people have been led to abusive behavior, committing acts of cruelty and great horror in the name of exorcising demons for Christ. Mothers have gone to jail for literally roasting their "possessed" infants in ovens to save them from the devil.[8] Parents have been known to chain a child in a room of their home so the child will not be tempted by Satan's legions "in the world."[9] Beating the devil out of a child, and occasionally an adult, is a common activity among extremist religious groups founded on the often-distorted teachings of a charismatic leader.[10]

Many modern-day televangelists might be said to use money to exorcise the devil. Some televangelists claim that a financial contribution to their ministry will be blessed by God. Some even list minimum suggested contributions when someone wishes healing from cancer, heart disease, and various other ailments.[11] Sometimes the disease is named. Sometimes the reference is to "the demon of sugar" (diabetes) or "the demon of breast cancer." The implication is that God heals through the exorcising power of money contributed to a minister who then uses his greater pipeline to the Almighty and prays away the problem.

Several fringe religious groups maintain the belief that mental illness, and possibly some physical infirmities or ailments, directly relate to demons.[12] Periodically there are arrests of extremist ministers and family members who have prayerfully whipped a mentally ill person in order to rid the person of the demons that are causing the problem.[13]

In most of the cases that have gone through the courts, the religious leader and family members do not feel that they are hurting the person who is possessed.[14] They acknowledge the screams and the fact that the person's skin may show signs of violence. But they claim that the screams are actually those of the demon, and the skin changes are an illusion created by the demon to force them to stop. Once the demon is exorcised, the child or mentally ill adult will be physically fine, happy, with no signs of the torture. Tragically the person is often disfigured or dies from the abuse before the authorities become aware of the misguided effort to "heal."[15]

EXORCISM

The result of all this confusion is great variation in the way exorcisms have been and are performed by those trying to be faithful to biblical teachings. Some exorcists firmly believe that demons cause mental illness or physical disability. Others feel that some mentally ill people believe they are demon possessed and change their behavior following an exorcism because they come to believe that the demons are no longer in control. And still other exorcisms are almost overlooked aspects of rituals such as baptisms and adult reaffirmations of baptismal rites.[16]

Not that congregations always are aware of such exorcisms in churches such as the Catholic and Episcopal churches. The wording seems just vague enough so the true meaning of what is being said is sometimes missed. For example, the church member may state that he or she renounces the powers of darkness and embraces the powers of light, that he or she renounces Satan and all his works. These words are exorcisms, yet they seem so simple that those speaking forget the power they have when invoking the name of God.

The degree of belief in the possibility of demon possession can be seen in the fact that the Catholic Church has for many years maintained designated exorcists in dioceses throughout the United States. And while rites of exorcism are relatively rare within the church, they continue to be held around the country as the need is perceived.

A well-known Episcopalian author of religious, psychology, and general interest books tells this experience he had with the forces of evil and a mentally ill woman.

> I had been working with a woman who was ritualistically abused as a child. Her father was head of a Satanic cult, and the child had been sexually used in services until she was thirteen years old. At that time, she had been impregnated by her father during a service where the [cult members] believed her father was used as an instrument of the devil. Her baby, supposedly Satan's child, was sacrificed, the heart and blood consumed by the group.
>
> The woman's story was confirmed independently by both a gynecologist who examined her and law-enforcement officers who had arrested and convicted various members of her father's group. She became emotionally disturbed, convinced that she was to be ritualistically sacrificed as the bride of Satan when she turned twenty-eight. The group wanted to use her in this manner, a fact borne out by independent law-enforcement agencies, but if she could not get with the group at the time of her birthday, she was to commit suicide.
>
> I had been working with her, getting her counseling and protection from the cult. However, despite all precautions, she did make a suicide effort. She was found in time, her stomach pumped of the drugs and alcohol she had consumed, and when I saw her in the hospital bed, I instinctively knew she would never try again. For some reason, the suicide attempt had been the last break with the cult, and she would be able to get on with her life. Although she could not return to where she had once lived until she

passed her twenty-eighth year, she and I both knew she would not be at risk again. In a sense, it could be said that we had beaten the devil.

I left the woman and went back to my office—actually a small two-bedroom apartment which had been converted into an outer area (the living room) for my secretary, a library, and my office. Everything seemed normal until I entered the area I used, the place that held my computer, my reference books, various awards I had earned over the years . . . everything that was personal.

Suddenly I felt the presence of evil. It was like when I was driving early one morning in the northwestern United States near the Pacific Ocean. There was a dense, moist fog that you could feel as well as see.

The evil felt like that. Not that I could see it. But I would swear I could feel it, like something dense, heavy, too thin to slow my movements, but present nonetheless.

My first thought was that this was hilarious. If this is what evil is really like, how impotent it must be. God makes mountains, and evil is a thick fog. Later I realized that, had I been scared, the outcome might have been very different. I don't know why I say that. I just sensed that my fear would give it power because it would separate me from what I had always professed, that God and God's love were always more powerful than anything related to the dark side of existence.

In any case, I laughed. Then, and this part is a little uncomfortable for me because I'm not from a religious background that normally does something like this, I said aloud, "In the name of Jesus, get out!"

That was when it dissipated. It was as if it was a cloud of dust being sucked steadily into a vacuum. I still couldn't see anything, and I certainly didn't hear anything, but the feeling of the fog was gone. Completely gone.

Later, when I got to thinking about what happened, I returned to the office, and still feeling a little foolish, walked through each room, asking God to bless it. I touched walls in every room, even the bathroom, repeating the prayer. I never had any problems again, though I also never talked about what occurred. I still feel a little funny mentioning it, but the exorcism, if that's what it was, seemed to work.[17]

How Are Exorcisms Performed?

But how are healing exorcisms performed? And when are they used? The answers vary, though some standard techniques are found throughout the country.

"I believe that good health is the natural state of humanity," said a nondenominational minister of a predominantly Hispanic church. "It's like that sign that says, 'God don't make junk.' Now sometimes people are hurting inside because of the actions of others. This state [Arizona] has one of the highest levels of child abuse in the nation, and those children are hurting because their parents are hurting and don't know how to love and nurture.

"And there are people who are shot or stabbed. Our inner cities are filled with people like that.

"And some people abuse themselves by eating all the wrong things, not taking care of themselves, not praising the Lord through their respect for their own bodies. You remember that we were made in the image of God, so when we abuse ourselves, we're defiling His temple.

"Now all these people need healings, and I think the Lord works those healings through psychologists and surgeons and nutrition experts. He could just as easily perform one of His miracles, but He wants us to reach out to one another or to use the skills that He has taught us.

"There's another kind of sickness, though. That's when the person does everything right, leads a good life, respects God's holy temple, and still that person comes down with the cancer or heart disease or something else. Now I don't believe that such illness is of God. That's Satan's work, trying to destroy a righteous man like he did with Job.

"What I do when one of my parishioners is possessed by Satan's handiwork, I go and I perform an exorcism in the name of Jesus. I just go right up to the bedside, and I *command* that demon to come out. I *command* that cancer to heal. And I visualize the love of Jesus washing over the sickness, driving out the demon, healing whatever was damaged.

"And I have them pray, too. I have them visualize being washed in the blood of the Lamb. But what's important is that I speak with His authority."[18]

Do the exorcisms work?

"Sometimes they do. And sometimes that demon's been possessing the mortal flesh for too long. That's when the healing comes from within. That's when God lets the physical body rot away, healing the heart and preparing the way for Heaven.

"I had one young woman, beautiful sister, a loving wife and mother. She was possessed by demons made manifest in what the doctors called leukemia. She knew better, of course. And so did I. But it was too late. The body is weak, meant to fall apart, because that way we know that the soul is the essence of God. The soul is His immortal self in us. And her body was just as weak as her spirit was strong.

"I prayed for her. I called out the demons. I saw them struggling within her, tormenting her with pain. And then there was this smile that came across her face. It was like what I imagine the Virgin Mary's face looked like at the moment she first saw our Lord emerge from her womb. And she said, 'It's all right. I've seen Jesus. I can die in peace.'

"Now to me, that was as much of an exorcism as when the demons come spewing forth from the mouth of the afflicted."[19]

During one healing session I attended, I witnessed a remarkable scene. Some of the participants in the session prayed for the power of the Lord to come through them to the afflicted person. They wanted to be conduits for his loving majesty, and they felt that when they laid hands on the person and prayed together, their request to God was strengthened. Other participants in the session, however, believed that the person's disease was the result of demon possession. I listened to them say prayers demanding the demons to free the afflicted person. Here were two groups, each of them viewing the illness and healing in a different way, yet they worked together.

Later, when I was able to talk with some of the people who participated, I found that each was skeptical of the other's methods. Still, they all felt that the end result would be the same, God's love would have the power to heal. In the end it didn't matter whether the person was possessed by demons or simply suffering from one of the ailments to which humans fall prey. What mattered was that God's power would prevail.

As we have said before in this section, healing is a mystery, a holy mystery not to be taken lightly or abused for personal gain or ego satisfaction. As we attempt to discern the abuses from the authentic, an examination of the historical development of healing, the church, and medical science will help us recognize misunderstandings, false teachings, and abuses that persist in our contemporary culture.

Part II
Historical Reflections on Healing

6

Healing Practices in Biblical Times

To gain some perspective of contemporary healing and faith-healing practices, the next few chapters will examine the historical roots of faith healing. Let's first turn attention to the healing practices prevalent during biblical times.

The Old Testament Israelite community saw God as a healer. The psalmist declared, "Praise the Lord, O my soul ... who heals all your diseases" (Ps. 103:2–3). And they recognized healing as more than mere physical healing. Proverbs, for example, speaks of emotional healing: "Reckless words pierce like a sword, but the tongue of the wise brings healing" (Prov. 12:18).

During the Israelites' forty-year period in the desert, they received this promise from God: "If you listen carefully to the voice of the Lord your God and do what is right in his eyes, if you pay attention to his commands and keep all his decrees, I will not bring on you any of the diseases I brought on the Egyptians, for I am the Lord who heals you" (Exod. 15:26).

Note that the freedom from disease was contingent on the Israelites' obedience to God's commands and decrees. Some of these commands were spelled out in the Levitical laws. For instance, people who suffered from a contagious skin disease were to follow specific instructions. "The person . . . must wash his clothes, shave off all his hair and bathe with water; then he will be ceremonially clean. After this he may come into the camp, but he must stay outside his tent for seven days. On the seventh day he must shave off all his hair; he must shave his head, his beard, his eyebrows and the rest of his hair. He must wash his clothes and bathe himself with water and he will be clean" (Lev. 14:8–9).

To many early Jews, wellness related to cleanliness rituals found both in the Torah (the first five books of the Old Testament) and the later rabbinical writings of the Talmud. Rituals served three purposes. They were used to prevent illness, to cure those who were sick, and to fulfill the ceremonial offerings required after recovery.

PREVENTIVE MEASURES

The Talmud has extensive explanations about the rules for good health, especially about the need for cleanliness and washing of one's hands before taking food. Writers of the Talmud went so far as to make statements like this one: "Whoever eats bread without first washing his hands is as though he had sinned with a harlot. Whoever makes light of the washing of his hands will be uprooted from the world. Whoever eats bread without scouring his hands is as though he eats unclean bread."[1]

Beliefs

It is easy to misread the intentions of the early health beliefs as being grounded in valid science of the day. Today we understand the transmission of germs and understand the importance of washing before eating. We know why it's essential to clean a cup before passing it to another person for a drink. We understand the problems, including colon cancer, that can be aggravated, at least in part, by irregular bowel movements. Thus Talmudic regulations that relate to such matters seem to strengthen the idea that Old Testament people had a grasp of contemporary health concerns.

Yet the early rabbis whose writings have been collected in the Talmud went much further, in ways that modern medical science now considers to be nonsense. For example, one of the teachings instructs: "If, upon awakening, you do not wash your hand before touching your body, you will go deaf or blind, and you will develop a sore." Or another rabbi admonished: "Uncleanliness of the head leads to blindness, uncleanliness of clothes leads to insanity, uncleanliness of the body leads to ulcers and sores; so beware of uncleanliness."[2]

Blood was also a focus for those concerned with health. The early Hebrews believed that skin disease was directly related to an overabundance of blood. It was thought that, for the first forty years of life, adults should be involved in bloodletting every month.[3] This need diminished with age, however, probably because it was felt that bloodletting, for the short term, reduced one's vigor and required a good meal for restoration. Since the elderly were already less vigorous, they dared not lose blood as often as a young person would.

The first meal to be consumed following the bloodletting also had specific connections with health. Meat was eaten to replace the lost flesh (as was believed to have occurred during the letting). And wine was to be consumed, since it was red in color and thus replaced red blood. Other foods, such as dairy products and poultry, were not to be eaten, and sexual intercourse was to be avoided. The latter was a serious problem since it was believed that death would occur if you had sex on the day that immediately followed the bloodletting.

Sleep was important, though the Talmud is clear about when someone must sleep and the consequences of a variance. Sleeping was to be at night, and sleeping through dawn made a man healthy and invigorated. It was unhealthy to sleep during the daytime for more than the time it would take to complete sixty normal breaths. The sixty breaths were considered to be the equivalent of a horse's nap. If a person avoided sleep for three days, death was sure to follow.[4]

The Talmud designated bread as critical to the human diet. It was believed that humans could not concentrate until they had eaten bread, perhaps with other food, and had something to drink. But there was also a belief that bread protected the body from demons and harmful spirits. Likewise, eating bread enabled someone to learn/teach the Torah, to win lawsuits, to maintain good breath, and even to stay in a monogamous marital relationship rather than lusting after other women. In fact, the regular consumption of bread assured that there would be no envy in a man's heart. Rather, he would be open to love.[5]

Water was the most critical of beverages and had to be consumed following the drinking of any other liquid. It was believed that when water entered the stomach, the food would float, preventing indigestion.

Over the centuries, the various rabbis developed their own beliefs about food and liquid. For example, one rabbi wrote that eaten food would rot and foul breath would occur unless the person followed any eating by walking at least four cubits. This specific distance seems rather odd when you consider that a cubit was equal to 17.5 inches; the walk was two fairly short steps.[6]

Some rabbis taught that eighty-three diseases (un-named) could be avoided by drinking a jug of water with salted bread every morning. The latter statement may have been made to assuage the feelings of the poor, for whom salt bread was often the only meal possible.[7]

The rabbis also designated how a person should buy food. People who had no money were to eat salted bread. Those with some money (usually a hundred shekels was the designated minimum, the amount also called a "mana") were to buy vegetables. Those who had a thousand shekels (ten mana) were also to buy fish. Five thousand shekels assured that meat could be purchased. And ten thousand shekels not only allowed the daily purchase of meat but also the privilege of hiring a cook. Regardless of wealth, however, it was important never to eat more meat than was needed to stop hunger. And if meat or vegetables could be afforded only once each week, then those foods were to be consumed only for the Sabbath.[8]

The majority of the people were able to afford only vegetables, so many of the Talmudic writings relate to vegetables and health. Again, such writings in some ways seem to reflect what we still read about nutrition and health. Other information, however, reflects superstition common in early biblical times and in later folk medicines.

CURATIVE MEASURES

The same is true with the treatment of existing ailments. Early faith healers believed that they should demand of God what God stated in the Torah. This action upset many rabbis, who saw such actions as arrogant. For example, some of the early Talmudic writers warned that it was wrong to try to heal by quoting scripture over a wound.

Typical were those healers who used part of Exodus 15:26, which states: "I will not bring on you any of the diseases I brought on the Egyptians, for I am the Lord, who heals you."

There were many reasons for the anger against those who used biblical incantations. The Exodus promise, for instance, is preceded by several requirements: *"If you listen carefully to the voice of the Lord your God and do what is right in his eyes, if you pay attention to his commands and keep all his decrees,* I will not bring on you any of the diseases I brought on the Egyptians, for I am the Lord, who heals you" (emphasis added). The promise required action by the people of God. Healing was not an automatic gift.

Oddly, the use of biblical verses, usually from Exodus, when used in healing ritual but not spoken directly to the injury or manifestation of disease (swelling, sores, etc.) seemed to be permitted. For example, the Talmud states:

> For inflammatory fever take a knife which is entirely made of iron, go to a place where there is a wild rose-bush, and tie a white twisted cord on it. On the first day let him cut a notch in it and say, "And the angel of the Lord appeared unto him in a flame of fire." On the morrow let him cut another notch and say, "And Moses said, I will turn aside now and see this great sight." The next day he cuts another notch and says, "And when the Lord saw that he turned aside." A Rabbi remarked, He should likewise say, "And He said, Draw not night hither." Consequently on the first day he should recite, "And the angel of the Lord appeared unto him . . . and Moses said"; on the second day, "And when the Lord saw"; and on the third day, "And he said, Draw not night hither." As he finishes this, let him bow low and cut it off, exclaiming, "O bush, O bush! not because thou wast loftier than all other trees did the Holy One, blessed be He, cause his *Shechinah* to alight upon thee, but because thou wast the lowliest of all the trees did He cause His *Shechinah* to alight upon thee. As thou didst see the fire of Hananiah, Mishael, and Azriah and flee from it, so see the fever of

[name of sufferer] son of [name the mother of the sufferer] and flee from it."

Note that only the mother's name could be cited for this fever treatment to work. If the incantation was not done precisely as written, instead of a single recitation, healing came only after forty-one repetitions.[9]

Some of the healing methods the rabbis taught were rather unpleasant. For example, to treat lacerated flesh, a person was instructed to take earth "from the shaded part of a privy," carefully mix it with honey, and eat it. It was believed that this treatment would lessen the pain of the open sores and accelerate the healing.[10]

One cure for weakness of the heart involved a mixture of cattle excrement dropped in the month of Nisan (April–May) and the right flank of a ram. The excrement was used as fuel for a fire to roast the ram's leg. Then the meat was eaten with diluted wine.[11]

A close reading of the various early cures seems to indicate that the different rabbis believed in whatever seemed to work. When a person came to them with a problem, they would try the remedies based either on the Torah or on the interpretations of the Torah. Then, if the sufferer got well, everyone was happy. If the sufferer didn't get well, the rabbis would sometimes experiment with variations of whatever it was that had been tried in the past. Or in the case of the weakened heart, if the appropriate cattle droppings could not be cultivated, willow twigs could be substituted. And if their action seemed to work, the "cure" was duly noted and taught to others.[12]

The rabbis enjoyed more success than a modern person might think would be possible. I see two possible reasons for this. First, many people felt better just having someone care about them. Some were not sick at all, suffering from loneliness or depression that was lifted when the rabbi took them seriously and helped them any way he could. Second, many conditions went into what we know today as spontaneous remission. For some period of time, the sufferer felt healthy and more comfortable. If that time immediately followed the ministrations of the rabbi or other healer, it was assumed that the healer was responsible for the regained health.

The same phenomenon occurs today. As one modern physician, a medical researcher, commented, "I'd never say this on the record, but the fact is that with all the advances we've made in medicine . . . most people—maybe 90 . . . 95 percent—most people either are going to get better or get worse no matter what a doctor does. And of those who get worse, most of them will have been made worse by the treatment. We call it iatrogenic illness in the hospital, but that word just means the doctor made a mistake, the patient reacted to the medication, or some other fool thing occurred that wouldn't have occurred if we geniuses had let well enough alone."[13]

While healing was a major concern of the early rabbis working from their interpretations of the Old Testament, especially the first five books of the Bible, most Christians tend to think of healing as most closely related to Jesus. In chapter 2, we have already looked at numerous miraculous healings Jesus performed. What is interesting to note is that some of the methods he used reflected cultural cures of the day.

For instance, human spittle was believed to be a cure for eye problems. According to the custom, the spittle had to come from the firstborn son of a father (though not the firstborn son of a mother if the father had previously had one or more sons). The gospel of Mark records two instances of Jesus using spittle to cure illness. First, in Mark 7, some people brought to Jesus "a man who was deaf and could hardly talk, and they begged him to place his hand on the man. After [Jesus] took him aside, away from the crowd,

Jesus put his fingers into the man's ears. Then he spit and touched the man's tongue. He looked up to heaven and with a deep sigh said to him, *'Ephphatha!'*(which means, 'Be opened!'). At this, the man's ears were opened, his tongue was loosened and he began to speak plainly" (Mark 7:32–35). In another account, Jesus spit on a blind man's eyes, touched him, and caused his sight to return (Mark 8:22–26).

Spittle could be used as either a curse or a cure. The Gospels record that when Jesus was questioned by the Sanhedrin before he was condemned to die, the questioners became disgusted with him. "They all condemned him as worthy of death. Then some began to spit at him, . . . [strike] him with their fists, . . . and beat him" (Mark 14:64–65). One story in the Talmud tells the humorous tale of one clever rabbi who used spittle in both ways to achieve a goal. The husband of a devoutly religious woman became angry with a rabbi. Feeling himself insulted, the husband insisted that his wife go and spit in the rabbi's face. Fearing to disobey her husband, yet respecting the learned teacher too much to disgrace him, the woman told the rabbi what was taking place.

The rabbi understood the dilemma. He didn't want her to act in a manner that was wrong for her, and at the same time he felt that she needed to respect her husband's wishes. Thinking quickly, he told her that he had been troubled of late with soreness of his eyes. He needed someone to spit in his eyes in order to heal them. He told her to spit so that he would be well.

Still frightened, yet understanding what the rabbi was trying to do for her, the woman obeyed. The rabbi insisted that she spit in his eyes seven times. The rabbi then told her to go home to her husband, and if the man asked her if she spit in the rabbi's face, she could truthfully say that she had done so, not once but seven times.[14]

Oddly, there was some basis for the idea of the healing power of spittle, a situation carried into modern times by superstitious people. It is known that certain early cultures made a stew-like dish into which the cook would spit. If she did not spit, the food upset the diners' stomachs. Experts today feel that the addition of spittle affected the enzyme action of the meal in some manner. Either it killed something harmful in the food, or it countered some problem.[15]

HEALING PRACTICES IN OTHER CULTURES OF THE TIME

The healing practices of other cultures in New Testament times was extremely primitive. The Romans considered themselves to be an advanced people, yet their methods were a step back from those of the Greeks, and the Greeks lacked sophistication.

Early Western cultures did not allow for a serious study of anatomy and physiology, the reasons varying with their religious beliefs. As a result, knowledge of healing came from guesswork and the repetition of what had worked in the past. For example, in Babylonia, it was common to keep the sick out in the open where passersby could notice their condition. It was hoped that someone going by would recognize symptoms similar to the ones he or she had endured at some previous time. When this occurred, the person would tell either the doctor or the sick person what had seemed to work. Thus "cures" might range from medicinal potions made from plants or herbs to religious ritual, such as a sacrifice to one of the gods.

Hippocrates, the Greek healer who is considered the father of modern medicine, relied on a more sophisticated approach. By the time he was practicing, the Greeks instructed all people who recovered from illness to go to the

temple of Aesculapius to have the story of their illness and
its remedies inscribed on a tablet. Hippocrates arranged for
all the tablets to be copied so the knowledge would be more
widely available. He was also able to compare symptoms
and remedies, finding preferred measures for treatment in a
crude version of contemporary pharmacological studies.

The ability to heal was considered a noble one, and
even the most important leaders of the day, such as
Alexander the Great, learned as much as they could.
Alexander, the most powerful military figure of his day,
took great pride in using roots to stop the bleeding and pain
of his friend Eurypylus when the latter was wounded in
battle.

The Roman writer Virgil talked of the gods providing
all healing powers in the form of plants found in gardens,
fields, and woods. All one had to do was learn what they
could do, and anything could be accomplished. Although
the idea existed for many generations, Hippocrates was the
man who restored the study, use, and cataloging of
remedies.

The Romans took most of their medicine from this
Greek background. The pagan religions, the Jewish faith,
and the emerging Christian tradition held physicians in high
regard for similar reasons. All religions that valued human
life felt that the loving care of people was the highest
calling. No matter what other religious practices existed,
and some could be quite brutal, most religions believed that
anything God (or one of the gods) created was the result of
a love that should be respected. Thus physicians, who
preserved life, were held in great respect, and the early
Christians often thought physicians were a vehicle for the
Holy Spirit.

Roman medical practitioners had come to understand
some basic principles of hygiene. The city of Rome was in
the midst of marshes that frequently flooded. Public

sanitation methods had to be carefully planned to avoid illness from human waste, mosquito-carrying diseases, and the like. As the culture developed, people's free time increased, much of it used for revelry. Diseases such as gout and syphilis became increasingly common by the first century.

Roman medicine that was not influenced by the Greeks relied on an odd mix of superstition, magic, and some ideas similar to the Old Testament healing beliefs. The Romans also used spittle to heal blindness and had physicians heal lameness through touching the healer's foot. When Roman citizens were ill, they brought offerings to the temples of Aesculapius and Minerva, and if the people were cured, they returned to the temples to bring gifts. They also were the first to develop what would today be called patent medicines.

As early as the first century B.C., the Romans were involved in a serious study of medicine, but they did not see the need to impose regulations on practitioners of healing arts. As a result, many dishonest tradesmen, seeing that people would buy any of the new remedies as long as someone implied the mixtures had healing powers, decided to make their own. Carpenters, shoemakers, and others created their own products from whatever was convenient rather than what was known to work. Many people were killed by the mixtures until the Roman officials began to regulate medical practice.

During this period, the Romans found themselves experiencing the same problems the Greeks had in trying to standardize treatment. Pliny the Elder, writing in his *Natural History,* quoted the Greek Cato, who had commented that their early physicians "seduce our wives, grow rich by feeding us poisons, learn by our suffering, and experiment by putting us to death."

Medical care varied drastically in Rome, though the

best physicians used methods we recognize today. Asclep-
iades of Prusa, a friend of Caesar, Antony, and other leaders
of the day, prescribed baths, wet compresses, enemas,
massage, exercise, diet, sunshine, abstinence from red meat,
and fasting to promote healing. He avoided the drastic
purges that were popular at the time, and only rarely relied
on drugs. He became one of the few physicians to have
success with such plagues as malaria, and he became famous
for successful throat surgery and for the loving care of the
insane.

Later, during the time of Vespasian, medical schools
were created, and the graduates, given the title of *medicus a
republica,* became the only legitimate physicians. Standards
were high, and carelessness, malpractice, or other failings
could be severely punished. Even childbirth, always a
practice of midwives, was studied, and the women were
given intense medical training to improve their skills.

By the first century A.D., military medicine had become
a separate practice and skill. Field ambulances were created,
along with the concept of first aid in the field. Twenty-four
physicians were routinely assigned to every legion, and
hospitals were maintained wherever the troops were quar-
tered for the long term.

The physicians also opened private hospitals, which
evolved into public care facilities by the Middle Ages. The
rich kept physicians on retainer or staff. The poor were
provided care by physicians paid by the state.

Within the first century A.D., medicine became more
specialized and women were extensively trained as doctors.
Every bodily function that was understood—urology, oph-
thalmology, dental care, and so forth—had a specialist. The
making of false teeth, bridge work, plates, and the like were
available. Even veterinarians were practicing in Rome.
Surgery had also been developed and was extremely skilled.
Doctors used anesthetics and over two hundred different

surgical instruments. Infection from bacteria, however, was not yet known, so deaths were common.

The use of drugs was greatly reduced during the first century A.D., but those that were used came from secret recipes known only to the physicians. This was not to prevent a return to the era of quack medicines. Rather it was to assure the highest possible fees. The medications came from common plants, so anyone knowing what they were could easily duplicate the treatment. Secrecy enabled the physicians to charge whatever they pleased for drugs, and the price escalated with the wealth of the sufferer. Strict ethical standards assured that no one was given a drug they did not need. However, there were no such standards for price, and the healing potions sold for whatever the market would bear.

In many ways the treatments—based on superstition, quackery, and pagan religious practices—were more dangerous than the problems. Little was known about mental illness, and almost nothing was known about anatomy and physiology.

7

The Healing Touch

Throughout history, healing powers have been associated with certain people. From early English and French documents, for instance, we learn that people looked to kings and queens to heal them.

THE ROYAL TOUCH

After witnessing Queen Elizabeth heal those afflicted with what was called the "King's Evil" during her visit to Gloucestershire in 1575, Robert Laneham wrote: "By her Highnes' accustomed mercy and charittee nyne cured of the peynfull and dangerous deseaz called the King's Evil; for that Kings and Queens of the Realm without other medicin save only by handing and prayers only doe cure it." These comments indicate that kings and queens were said to have cured people without using medicine, using only "handing" (touching) and prayer.

The following passage from William Shakespeare's *Macbeth* illustrates a similar perspective.

> *Malcolm:* ... Comes the King forth, I pray you?
>
> *Doctor:* Aye sir, there are a crew of wretched souls
> That stay his cure [that wait for him to heal them].
> Their malady convinces the great assay of art
> [their illness defeats the attempts of the medical art]
> but at his touch,
> Such sanctity hath Heaven given his hand,
> They presently [immediately] amend. . . .
>
> *Macduff:* What's the disease he means?
>
> *Malcolm:* 'Tis called the Evil.
> A most miraculous work in this good King,
> Which often, . . .
> I have seen him do. How he solicits Heaven, . . .
> But strangely visited people,
> All swoln and ulcerous, pitiful to the eye, . . . he cures,
> Hanging a golden stamp about their necks,
> Put on with holy prayers. And 'tis spoken,
> To the succeeding royalty he leaves
> The healing benediction.
>
> (Act IV, Scene III)

Both of these passages refer to an illness called the King's Evil or the Evil. This referred to a skin disease that was most obvious in the swollen necks of the sufferers, as well as through occasional scarring. The disease was later named scrofula, a condition now identified as tuberculosis of the lymphatic glands. It was known as the King's Evil not because the king had caused the illness but because it was the divine right of royalty to cure it through touch.

King Edward, the Fraud

Unfortunately, one of the early English kings used his "healing" power in a fraudulent way. Edward the Confessor, king in 1051, realized that healing could be used as a way of assuring power at a time when his throne was in jeopardy. He circulated this story throughout the land:

> A young woman had married a husband of her own age, but having no issue by the union, the humours collected abundantly about her neck, she contracted a sore disorder, and the glands swelling in a dreadful manner. Admonished in a dream to have the part affected washed by the king, she entered the palace, and the king himself fulfilled the labour of love by rubbing the woman's neck with his fingers dipped in water. Joyous health followed his healing hand; the lurid skin opened, so that worms flowed out with the purulent matter, and the tumour subsided. Before a week had expired a fair new skin returned, and hid the scars so completely that nothing of the original wound could be discovered.[1]

But the most rudimentary knowledge of anatomy and biology indicates that the description of Edward the Confessor's act is a medical impossibility. Failure to give birth to a child does not result in the swelling of a woman's neck or in worms and "purulent matter" that has to be released.

The king was not a fool; he knew the story was preposterous. He thus arranged with the court physicians to establish the first formal faith-healing program designed to boost his image with the masses.

The king's methods were quite sophisticated. He knew his physicians could identify certain common ailments, such as scrofula, even if they could not cure these ailments. He and his physicians also knew that the large ugly boils that accompanied scrofula would burst, drain, and heal if they were left alone. The trained eye of the physicians knew when the boils were about to rupture.

King Edward the Confessor announced and arranged an elaborate ceremony during which he would use his "divine gift" to "heal" those with scrofula. When the afflicted people arrived, they would first be examined by the court physicians. The doctors would assure that anyone who truly had scrofula or some other long-term illness would be declared not ready to see the king. Only those with large boils about to erupt would be touched. Then, when they broke, oozed, and healed (as would occur no matter what was done), the king received the credit for another miraculous cure.

English and French Royal Healers

Both the French and English royalty engaged in healing activities, though the English carried on the tradition far longer. It is not known if others were aware of Edward the Confessor's cheating, though it is certain that, even if they did, a few of the monarchs truly believed they had healing power.

There were many different approaches to healing the King's Evil. Generally a coin was used in the ceremony. In some ceremonies the coin served as the admission ticket given to those in line as the item the monarch would use to touch the ill part of the person's body. In other ceremonies the coin became the blessed souvenir given to the people after they had gone through the healing line.

Frequently the king or queen would use the coin to make the sign of the cross on or over any swelling or sores. Some people would take advantage of these "healing" services to collect the coins, using them to pay for food and shelter. Some people made a reasonable living by being "healed" every time a king or queen performed the ceremony.

Queen Anne, uncomfortable with the physical closeness, used her ring for touching. Elizabeth, on the other hand, would often touch directly. Elizabeth also did not want the British people to think that the royal family's break with Catholicism prevented God from working through their hands. She needed to establish that she could provide divine intervention with or without the pope's approval.

Elizabeth (1533–1603) had been an enthusiastic "healer" at first, pressing her fingertips into open sores while praying sincerely. The idea that she should sully her hands so upset the royal doctors that they would sometimes place a plaster over a particularly gruesome running sore so she would not have such direct contact. Over time, however, she recognized that many of the people she touched were not getting well. She also wondered if such curing was against the law.

Elizabeth finally stopped touching, then returned to the act toward the end of the sixteenth century for reasons best explained by a physician-biographer. He wrote: "Queen Elizabeth did, for some time, discontinue the Touching for the King's Evil, doubting either the Success or Lawfulness, of that way of Curing. But She soon quitted that Fitt of Puritanisme, when the Papists defamed her, as if God had withdrawn from her the gift of Healing, because she had withdrawn herself from the Roman Church."

The Catholics, well aware that Elizabeth had been excommunicated by the pope, watched her healing with respect. They believed in her abilities, then decided that the healing took place despite Elizabeth. She always used the sign of the cross, and it was that sign, the Catholic critics alleged, that brought forth the healing. Although Elizabeth firmly believed in God's power to heal, including through her touch, she avoided touching during the plague of 1562. King James avoided healing during the summer months, issuing a statement in 1616 that the sick could not come to him between Easter and Michaelmas.

Charles I tried to follow suit, but he was faced with a plague in May, 1626, and was forced to begin trying to heal his subjects. Unlike his predecessors, he felt obligated to touch regardless of the disease when a crisis arose. His personal belief, however, was that royal healing was certain only in the case of the King's Evil.

Sir Francis Drake wrote of watching the king's touching

in April of 1639: "During the tyme the King touched those that had the disease called the Evil, were read these words: 'They shall lay their hands upon the sick and they shall recover.' During the tyme the King put about every of their necks an angel of gold [a coin equal in value to a physician's pay] with a white ribben, were read these words: 'That Light was the true light which lighteth every man which cometh into the world.'"

It was under Charles I that the public most frequently began seeking his "help" only to obtain the coin. The belief in the power of the king to heal had diminished for many. Those believers who sought his help, however, showed their convictions of God's special blessing when Charles was taken prisoner during the Civil War. A blind woman came to Charles, begging for help. He informed her that he had no gold coin to give her, believing the woman to be one of the people who used the "touch pieces," as the coins were called, to supplement her meager income. Instead, the woman begged that he would touch her in the name of Jesus Christ, a request he could not ignore. Three days later she could see again.

In another story, a man on crutches brought his own coin, a shilling, to the Isle of Wight, where Charles I was staying. The lame man was able to walk after three days. Three weeks later "he was able to play nine pins and run after his Bowl," and within the year he had become a sailor in Newfoundland.

Some people believed that royalty could also cure cases of the plague through touch. Peter of Blois, an archdeacon of London, wrote between 1170 and 1180: "I admit indeed that it is a sacred duty to attend upon the lord King: for he is holy and the Lord's Anointed, nor has he received the sacrament of royal unction in vain, as if its efficacy be not known or be in doubt the disappearance of bubonic plague and the cure of scrofula will beget the fullest belief."

The various kings and queens of England were not so foolish as to try and cure *any* disease, especially if they felt it might be contagious. Those who believed in their special healing powers limited their actions to real or alleged cases of scrofula. And some who did not believe simply refused to get involved. William III of England never touched, and it was said of William the Conquerer that he lacked the time to heal the sick because he was too busy killing those who were healthy. William III thought the matter was nonsense but went along with the action much as a modern politician might attend a supermarket opening. His scorn was obvious when he touched each person while saying the words, "May God give you better health and more sense."

Doctors working during the time of Charles II were excused for their inability to cure patients. Anytime they had a problem, they simply sent the patient to the king to be touched. In that way, they were using a specialist and avoided possible charges of malpractice. Unfortunately this meant that so many people sought the king's touch that he finally had to insist that people brought certificates from their "Minister and Church Wardens [where they live] that they never were touched by His Majesty before."

France's Louis XIII was only nine years old when he began healing. The year was 1610, and he had just assumed the French throne. Taking the task seriously, the boy king began fasting the night before he was to "heal." On the day of his coronation, he was reported to have touched between 800 and 900 people and would frequently "heal" 1,000 or more at a time during his reign.

Louis XIV (1638–1715) was taken to the priory of St. Marcoul de Corbeny near Reims, France, after his coronation in 1643. There he touched a minimum of 2,600 people, approximately three times the number his predecessor touched during his coronation.

Royalty was considered to be divinely blessed. At the

very least, the public believed that God acted through royalty. At the extreme, they believed that the powers of their kings and queens were little different from those of Jesus.

The belief in the healing power of royalty has diminished in recent years. But the idea of someone walking in our midst, acting as God's representative, or at least having special power presumably from God, remains a popular one.

OBJECTS THAT HEAL

It was during these same periods in history that people began to believe that certain objects had the power to heal. Some of these ideas evolved rather naturally. When the Greeks introduced coins into their culture, for instance, they engraved on the sides of the coins the faces of their gods. It wasn't long, however, before the faces on the coins looked more like the rulers than the gods. And by the time of Alexander the Great, the faces of the rulers replaced the faces of the gods.

Many people believed that if the ruler had power to heal, then the coin with his or her face engraved on it might also have the power to heal. Especially coveted were the coins used in healing. When the people obtain one of these "touch pieces," they ascribed to it all the healing properties supposedly held by the king or queen who had used it for touching.

For example, one story tells of an ill man who had been given a gold coin by Charles I. He wore the coin around his neck, believing it gave him continuing health. Years after Charles I was beheaded, the man had a son. When the son fell ill, the father loaned him the touch piece Charles I had given to him. The son immediately recovered. As a result, the two men alternated wearing the coin, depending on which man felt himself with "distemper."

Or people saved other relics belonging to kings or queens they believed had healing powers. For example, when Charles I was executed, some men took the shirt the king had worn and claimed it to be a sacred garment that was capable of curing scrofula. For many years those who were truly ill would seek the shirt's curing power.

THE HEALING TOUCH TODAY

Some of the practices in contemporary healing services are reminiscent of the royal touch. A television program I watched last week demonstrates my point.

After the crusade speaker had finished her teaching time, members of the audience came forward and stood in a long line across the front of the auditorium. The evangelist began at one end of the line and touched each person on the forehead, giving each a gentle shove. Behind each person in the line, people designated as "catchers" were ready to catch the person if he or she responded to the evangelist's touch by falling backward. The evangelist said something to each person as she touched his or her forehead, but the television microphones did not pick up what she was saying. From my experience in witnessing similar services, she may have been saying something like, "In the name of Jesus Christ, be healed." When the evangelist had touched each person in the line, a new line of people formed, each person waiting for the healing touch of the evangelist.

This phenomenon, often known as the "slaying in the Spirit" or being "slain in the Spirit," reminds me of the stories of king's and queen's subjects lining up to receive the royal touch. People seek the touch of a healer.

The techniques used vary from group to group. I have seen slayings in the Spirit in Beverly Hills churches as well as in small rural churches in poverty-stricken areas of the country. In some services, the touch is gentle; in others it is more like a shove. In some services the people touched by the minister or evangelist fall back slightly; in others the person falls back completely and is lowered to the floor. Those on the floor may go rigid or limp. They may pray, speak praise words, speak in tongues, move about on their backs, have a look of ecstasy on their faces, or seem to be catatonic.

In some services the people are helped to their feet and return to their seats. In a few healing services conducted by a professional healer passing through the community, I have noticed that the people are led out through a back way. This allows for faster "slayings," and it also assures that someone who seems to overreact can be quietly taken outside.

Reactions to the touch and the slaying in the Spirit vary. Some people I spoke to feel it's a part of the healing process or a reaffirmation of faith, a way of gaining closeness to God. And others seem to view it as a ritual that is important for them, though they are uncertain why.

"I just feel better after it," said one woman. "There is such a sense of love up there. Everybody being slain in the Spirit. Everybody on that floor, praising the Lord. It's as if Jesus is right there with us, jolting our souls into working even harder for his kingdom. I don't know if it really changes my life, but I can tell you my spiritual life would be a little empty without the experience."

Other people have their doubts. Elizabeth, now a physician in the Southwest, tells this story: "My father and I went to a healing service where there was a call to come forward and be slain in the spirit. I don't know why he took me. I guess he didn't want to go alone. But I didn't believe in such things. I was a good little Catholic girl like my mother. There wasn't even a charismatic Catholic movement back then, so I was pretty cynical about the whole thing.

"I know why my father went. He had been a deeply

troubled man since my mother was killed in an accident I always suspected was murder. He was a brutal man, but he had enough influence in the town that the police and the prosecutor never looked too hard at the case. I kept trying to tell them something was wrong, but I was only seven at the time, and no one would listen. After that, I hated my father, and he seemed wary of me, especially after I became a teenager the same age as Mom was when she and my father first started dating.

"Anyway, my father insisted that everything would be fine for us after he was slain in the Spirit. I didn't even know he believed in God, but I was either too afraid of him or too curious. . . I don't know which. . . So I went with him.

"I didn't go forward with him. I wasn't going to be a hypocrite. I just watched as one of these visiting evangelists prayed over him, then struck his forehead with the palm of his hand.

"My father fell backward into the arms of a couple of burly men who looked like body builders. They laid him on the floor where he began shouting that he was healed. By the time he got back to me, he was telling everyone how wonderful his life was going to be, how everything he had done wrong had been made right, how the future would be so great.

"It wasn't. Nothing changed. He took to too much drinking and womanizing, and I left home, working my way through college.

"I barely saw him after that, though there was one Christmas a year or two later when he was a little drunk and belligerent and I asked him about why he had to be so rotten after being slain in the Spirit. He wouldn't answer me."

Therapeutic Touch

Researchers who have studied the effect of human touch on ill people have discovered that therapeutic touching can be an important aspect of healing.[2] For example, it is now understood that the human body gives off an energy field that varies with one's health. It is also known that when an illness is localized, therapeutic touching of the area seems to cause a change in the hemoglobin, the factor that, among other things, carries oxygen from the lungs to the tissues of the body and carbon dioxide from tissues to the lungs. This change does not occur when touch is applied to a healthy body or to the healthy part of the body when illness is localized.[3]

Dr. Delores Krieger, a pioneer in touch therapy now taught to medical professionals, has theorized that a healthy person has an abundance of energy given off by the body and the sick person has a deficit. Touching enables a transfer of energy between healer and afflicted to take place.[4]

Touch has also been an important part of health care when the touch involves therapeutic massage. There are several forms of massage therapy, ranging from relaxation of muscles through manipulation of key points of the body to a series of smooth strokes worked in a prescribed direction. But no matter what the technique, several changes have been found to consistently result.

The lymphatic system flow is improved through massage, a fact that allows toxins to be cleansed from the human body. Circulation is improved through the dilation (opening) of the blood vessels. Muscle tension is reduced, and the person feels better following the massage.

Another form of therapeutic touch has been developed by Dr. Norman Harris as a way of releasing the body's beta endorphins to reduce or eliminate the effects of premenstrual stress in women.[5] Beta endorphins are natural pain killers that are released at times of both positive and negative stress. Runners talk of "hitting the wall," a moment when suddenly they stop hurting, stop feeling the strain of their efforts, and can continue with relative comfort, all because of beta endorphin release. These pain killers are released during physical exercise, childbirth, sexual intercourse, and at other times. And they can be deliberately released through therapeutic touch.

The healing touch. Whether that touch has come from royalty, a minister, a faith healer, a compassionate medical professional, or a therapist—people through the centuries have sought the healing touch. Does God give special power to certain people to touch and heal? Some physicians may say that the laying on of hands brings emotional reassurance to a patient, but little more. Other people believe that the laying on of hands for faith healing transfers God's power to the ill person.

Whether God works through the hands of those who touch or whether the touching helps to release natural curative powers of the body as designed by our Creator is not important. What is important is that God can and has used human touch to heal people's illnesses. As with any of the other techniques we have discussed, this aspect of healing is open to fraudulent use by people who through ego needs, greed, or other reasons abuse the process by asserting that their human touch alone can cure a person's illnesses. Once again we look at the people who have been restored by a healing touch, and we admit the mystery of the healing process.

8

Mesmer and Christian Science

One of the American religious groups most widely known for its practices of faith healing is the First Church of Christ, Scientist. Christian Science has some of its beginnings with Friedrich Anton Mesmer, a man whose healing approach became popular in France in 1784.

MESMER

Mesmer was a figure both praised and damned for his ideas, which were eccentric enough to prevent him from gaining a medical license in Vienna, Berlin, and Paris. He was eventually able to begin practicing in France, however, by going into partnership with Dr. Charles Delson. He worked under Delson's license, a legal situation at the time.

Mesmer's research has led him to be credited as a

forerunner of psychotherapy. He had a crude understanding of the power of suggestion and the fact that people could be influenced by their subconscious. Mesmer was able to help people relax, to talk about their problems, and to find solutions through guided discussions that led to emotional healing and occasional physical healing.

James Wykoff's book *Franz Anton Mesmer: Between God and Devil* (Englewood Cliffs, N.J.: Prentice Hall, 1975) tells us that Mesmer did not understand that his success came from the interaction with patients. Instead, he believed that his cures were caused by animal magnetism and required elaborate rituals and special equipment.[1]

Mesmer's approach was, in some ways, the forerunner of contemporary hypnotherapy, which brings subjects to a highly relaxed state in which their minds are open to suggestion. But Mesmer was convinced that he was tapping into the power of the universal fluid that he believed exists in all of nature. According to this belief, the fluid's effect is passed from healer to patient by animal magnetism.

The presentations of Mesmer's theories were often done in groups, Mesmer handling them like a show. He placed a tub in the center of the room and had his patients stand around the tub. Iron rods, jointed so they could be bent to whatever angle was necessary to touch the afflicted portion of the patient's body, were inserted in the tub through holes. It was the tub that would supposedly gather the animal magnetism.

Cords linked together each of the ill people standing around the tub. In addition, patients made a link with the people standing on either side of them by interlocking their thumbs and forefingers into the circles made by the other patients' thumbs and forefingers.

Mesmer would use music to bring the patients into harmony with the animal magnetism. Either a musical instrument was played or people sang.

Over the course of what usually was several hours, either Dr. Delson or Mesmer would walk around the patients, touching them with an iron rod. By the end of each session, many of the women and some of the men were convulsing. They would laugh, cry, and generally carry on.

Mesmer was able to obtain large sums of money from the people who came to him, claiming he would use it to build a hospital and to fund his own scientific academy. On March 12, 1784, however, the king of France began to be suspicious of Mesmer's work and ordered an investigation by nine of the leading scientists of the day, including Dr. Benjamin Franklin, who was in Paris working for the new transitional American government.

Franklin was an open-minded scientist who commented that the delusion caused by Mesmer's animal magnetism "may, however, in some cases be of use while it lasts. There are in every great rich city a number of persons who are never in health because they are fond of medicines and always taking them, whereby they derange the natural functions and hurt their constitutions. If these people can be persuaded to forbear their drugs in expectation of being cured by only the physician's finger or an iron rod pointing at them, they may possibly find good effects though they mistake the cause."[2]

The French investigative team felt that the reaction of Mesmer's subjects during their observation of his work was tainted by their presence in a room where normally only the patients and the healer worked together. They stopped observing and arranged for their own experiments, using Mesmer's procedures, conducting them in Franklin's home in Passy, France.

The subjects for the healings included men and women with tumors, swellings, blindness, and other disabilities. One test was made with seven people, four of whom claimed no change and three of whom said they felt a little better. Another test, involving four people, resulted in no change.

A third test started with Dr. Delson supposedly magnetizing an apricot tree that would then have curative powers that could be felt by the subject. For the test, a twelve-year-old boy was blindfolded, then told to find the magnetized tree, based on his physical reactions. The boy went to each of four unmagnetized trees in a line that led him further and further from the tree that had been magnetized. He claimed, however, that he could feel the power of the magnetism growing stronger with each tree he touched, his reaction to the "magnetic power" ranging from a headache to fainting.[3]

None of the tests indicated the presence of magnetism, special fluids, or anything else. The observations showed that the people seemed to respond to the physical touch of the healer, to the expectation of chance, and to the emotions that so theatrical a setting could trigger.

MARY BAKER EDDY

Mary Baker Eddy, the founder of Christian Science, was exposed to Mesmer's beliefs and practices through her teacher, Phineas Parkhurst Quimby, who had studied mesmerism as Mesmer developed it, aspects of hypnotism as it evolved from some of Mesmer's followers, and related concepts. He then created a healing practice with Mary as both a patient and a disciple.

This new approach to thinking and health appealed to Mary. Mesmerism as it was evolving at the time that Quimby was practicing also related to other ideas, including spiritualism. The United States was just beginning to gain an influx of immigrants such as the Irish who were bringing with them strong beliefs in demons, devils, and related ideas. Thus Mary's first education combined a number of related ideas that came from different disciplines popular in her day.

For example, many people believed that life contained many subtle influences that were quite different from what they seemed. Disease might not exist at all. Instead of being sick, an individual might either be suffering from thinking they were sick, or they might be influenced by demons. While Mary Baker Eddy would ultimately deny any such influences, however, her teachings have an obvious base in popular ideas of that era. Moreover, she was never quite so certain of her beliefs in her own life. She developed painful kidney stones and relied on morphine and other pain killers to ease her discomfort.

Oddly, Mary Baker Eddy later turned against mesmerism, claiming that any practice that so strongly involved the mind could also be used against her. She claimed that her third husband died as a result of "mesmeric poison," which acted much like arsenic but was not of the material world.

Mary Baker Eddy's Beliefs

Mary Baker Eddy believed that evil and illness were not real; they were the products of what she called "mortal mind." In contrast, "immortal Mind" or "divine Mind" was real; it was the only truth. "If you listen and react to the mortal mind, you will experience the *illusions* of doubt, depression, sickness, pain, anger and sadness. So you must reject the messages of mortal mind. . . . If mortal mind sends a message telling you how sick you feel, reject it. Pay attention only to immortal Mind, which instructs you that sickness is unreal."[4]

In her book *Science and Health with Key to the Scriptures,* the book that Christian Scientists consider to be an essential tool to understanding the Bible, Eddy says, "Man is never sick, for Mind is not sick and matter cannot be. A false belief is both the tempter and the tempted, the sin and the sinner, the disease and its cause. It is well to be calm in sickness; to be hopeful is still better; but to understand that sickness is not real and that Truth can destroy its seeming reality, is best of all, for this understanding is the universal and perfect remedy."[5]

Mary Baker Eddy believed that the immortal Mind needs no outside force to heal. Someone who utilizes the divine Mind is using the only power that matters, and thus no other issues related to contemporary medicine are important.

> It is plain that God does not employ drugs or hygiene, nor provide them for human use; else Jesus would have recommended and employed them in his healing. The sick are more deplorably lost than the sinning, if the sick cannot rely on God for help and the sinning can. The divine Mind never called matter *medicine,* and matter required a material and human belief before it could be considered as medicine.
>
> Sometimes the human mind uses one error to medicate another. Driven to choose between two difficulties, the human mind takes the lesser to relieve the greater. On this basis it saves from starvation by theft, and quiets pain with anodyns. You admit that mind influences the body somewhat, but you conclude that the stomach, blood, nerves, bones, etc., hold the preponderance of power. Controlled by this belief, you continue in the old routine. You lean on the inert and unintelligent, never discerning how this deprives you of the available superiority of divine Mind. The body is not controlled scientifically by a negative mind.[6]

Mrs. Eddy wrote in the "Recapitulation" section of her book *Science and Health with Key to the Scriptures:*

> The Scriptures inform us that man is made in the image and likeness of God. Matter is not that likeness. The likeness of Spirit cannot be so unlike Spirit. Man is spiritual and perfect; and because he is spiritual and perfect, he must be so understood in Christian Science. Man is idea, the image of Love; he is not physique. He is the compound idea of God, including all right ideas; the generic term for all that reflects

God's image and likeness; the conscious identity of being as found in Science, in which man is the reflection of God, or Mind, and therefore is eternal; that which has no separate mind from God; that which has not a single quality underived from Deity; that which possesses no life, intelligence, nor creative power of his own, but reflects spiritually all that belongs to his Maker. . . .

Man is incapable of sin, sickness, and death. The real man cannot depart from holiness, nor can God, by whom man is evolved, engender the capacity or freedom to sin. A mortal sinner is not God's man. Mortals are the counterfeits of immortals. They are the children of the wicked one, or the one evil, which declares that man begins in dust or as a material embryo. In divine Science, God and the real man are inseparable as divine Principle and idea.

Mrs. Eddy explained that

when man demonstrates Christian Science absolutely, he will be perfect. He can neither sin, suffer, be subject to matter, nor disobey the law of God. Therefore he will be as the angels in heaven. Christian Science and Christianity are one. How, then, in Christianity any more than in Christian Science, can we believe in the reality and power of both Truth and error, spirit and matter, and hope to succeed with contraries? Matter is not self-sustaining. Its false supports fail one after another. Matter succeeds for a period only by falsely parading in the vestments of law.[7]

Health, then, in Mary Baker Eddy's view is a spiritual reality. And healing is accomplished through spiritual understanding. If sickness is part of a false perception of reality, then healing comes when that falsehood is exposed to spiritual truth. "Healing is one of the natural results of drawing close to immortal Mind and resolving spiritual conflicts."[8]

Christian Science Practitioners

A Christian Scientist, then, responds to sickness by trying to find the spiritual truth. To help people in their search, the Mother Church, the First Church of Christ, Scientist in Boston, approves and trains people to be practitioners—people who pray for those who are ill.

Training is carefully controlled. All members study Mrs. Eddy's works and read some or all of the contemporary Christian Science publications. Anyone can become a healer through such study, though the practitioners, endorsed by the Mother Church, also study for ten days under a teacher who has been instructed by the Massachusetts Metaphysical College. (The graduates receive a Bachelor of Christian Science degree and may use the letters C.S.B. by their names). While this seems to imply intense learning, the college's course is seven days in length and repeated every three years. Although class work is intense and serious, the educational program is largely a self-taught mastery of Mrs. Eddy's writings along with Bible study guided both by Mrs. Eddy's work and various reference works that might be used by any Christian Bible student.

When Christian Scientists are ill, they find healing by reading Mary Baker Eddy's book *Science and Health with Key to the Scriptures.*

> When the illusion of sickness or sin tempts you, cling steadfastly to God and His idea. Allow nothing but His likeness to abide in your thought. Let neither fear nor doubt overshadow your clear sense and calm trust, that the recognition of life harmonious—as Life eternally is—can destroy any painful sense of, or belief in, that which Life is not. Let Christian Science, instead of corporeal sense, support your understanding of being, and this understanding will supplant error with Truth, replace mortality with immortality, and silence discord with harmony.[9]

Practicing Christian Scientists may also call for spiritual counsel and prayer from a practitioner. For instance, if a Christian Scientist falls and injures his ankle, he may call on a practitioner to come and pray with him. The practitioner will help the man understand that his ankle hurts only to the degree that he accepts the material evidence that he is injured. If he can control his negative thinking and concentrate only on the reality that he is a child of God, a perfect being, he will be healed.[10]

Practitioners are trained to view all illness as unreality. They believe that to recognize illness, to give it a name, is to give it a power. Denial is extremely important in order to heal. The Christian Scientist will not look to contemporary medicine, because to do so is to give the tumor or illness that much greater power. To the Christian Scientist, this is a strong act of faith that results in healing.

There is a logic to Christian Science's shunning of medicine based on the "Message to the Mother Church for 1901" in which Mary Baker Eddy said:

> If God created drugs for medical use, Jesus and his disciples would have used them and named them for that purpose, for he came to do "the will of the Father." . . . The divine Life, Truth, Love—whom men call God—is the Christian Scientists' healer; and if God destroys the popular triad—sin, sickness, and death—remember it is He who does it and so proves their nullity. Christians and clergymen . . . believe that divine power, besought, is given to them in times of trouble, and that He worketh with them to save sinners. I love this doctrine, for I know that prayer brings the seeker into closer proximity with divine Love, and thus he finds what he seeks, the power of God to heal and to save.[11]

From Mary Baker Eddy's point of view, taking medicine is almost an affront to God. Certainly it reflects a lack of faith in His ability to heal.

Illness and Health

Perhaps the greatest question the critics have of Christian Scientists is whether or not the beliefs work. For a member of the Christian Science Church, illness can be considered a spiritual failing, and retaining an illness definitely brings the sufferer's faith into question.

> Mind must be found superior to all the beliefs of the five corporeal senses, and able to destroy all ills. Sickness is a belief, which must be annihilated by the divine Mind. Disease is an experience of so-called mortal mind. It is fear made manifest on the body. Christian Science takes away this physical sense of discord, just as it removes any other sense of moral or mental inharmony. That man is material, and that matter suffers,—these propositions can only seem real and natural in illusion. Any sense of soul in matter is not the reality of being. . . .
>
> Is it not a species of infidelity to believe that so great a work as the Messiah's was done for himself or for God who needed no help from Jesus' example to preserve the eternal harmony? But mortals did need this help, and Jesus pointed the way for them. Divine Love always has met and always will meet every human need. It is not well to imagine that Jesus demonstrated the divine power to heal only for a select number or for a limited period of time, since to all mankind and in every hour, divine Love supplies all good.[12]

Some Christian Scientists believe that accidents, injuries, and ill health occur only if the person anticipates their occurrence. Matter becomes a projection of the mind, as do the negative experiences of the body. Taken to a logical extreme, then, physical death can be overcome, a situation which many Christian Scientists believe.

The problem with immortality comes from the tremendous thought process against such an event happening. This is called Consentaneous Thinking and represents the collective negative thoughts of those who still believe that life is finite. They relate such experience to the time when people thought the world was flat or limited to the horizons they could see from where they lived. As long as they lived their lives according to this Consentaneous Thought, the world might as well have been as limited as their beliefs. But when they challenged these ideas, a far greater world of experience was opened to them. Likewise, when the Consentaneous Thought concerning the limits of human existence is successfully challenged and changed, life as we know it will be vastly expanded, perhaps for eternity.[13]

Illness is the mind's projection of an improper thought. This is not to say that an adult practicing Christian Scientist is immune from the colds and flu that plague others. It is just that they recognize the cause, and when their thought process has been rectified, the illness will be over. Sometimes this correction occurs in the same length of time that the illness normally runs its course for the person who does not follow such a belief system. Sometimes the illness seems to be briefer or less severe. And sometimes it lingers longer than it might for someone seeking conventional medical treatment, though this is blamed on the projection of the sufferer, not the healing power of conventional medicine.

Although Christian Scientists basically reject medical treatment, they do involve medical people in childbirth and in setting broken bones. The setting of a broken bone, for instance, is not medicine in the sense that met with Mrs. Eddy's disapproval, and so the use of physicians toward this end is quite acceptable within the Christian Science Church.

George Channing, a Christian Science lecturer, teacher, and practitioner, notes, however, that "there are innumerable instances of bone fractures which have been set and healed perfectly under Christian Science treatment—without medical or surgical aid. Results depend upon honest effort, correct understanding and constancy in Christian Science practice. . . . If the Christian Scientist has not reached the degree of spiritual understanding which is needed for healing by spiritual means and resorts to some other means, he obviously cannot be said to be employing fully the method of Christian Science. He does not undergo condemnation for this; nor does he assume any burden of guilt. He is always free to improve his spiritual understanding and employ it exclusively, thus restoring his status as a Christian Scientist."[14]

One source of concern to skeptics of Christian Science practice lies in the ability to document the healings. In an attempt to present empirical evidence that prayer is the only true healer, church publications such as *An Empirical Analysis of Medical Evidence in Christian Science Testimonies of Healing 1969-1988* mention bone breaks that were identified by X ray, set, and then healed more rapidly than would be expected. Some of the breaks healed within twenty-four hours. Others took as long as a week or more. But all recoveries were documented, and all occurred days, weeks, or months earlier than would be expected through conventional medicine.

The Committee on Publication, however, which produces the literature read by the members, is comprised of members of the Christian Science Church. Frequently, they don't feel the need to include the kind of detail that an outside skeptic would want in order to cross-check the claim. For example, they mention "a fractured jaw, confirmed in writing by a dentist whose diagnosis was made in consultation with a physician" that "healed within one day." But when checking the end note that presumably provides the source, the reference is to *The Christian Science Journal,* (September 1965) 83:613–14. Since the publication is occasionally sent to the news media, a reference listing where the item was supposedly published rather than using a copy of the documentation of fracture and healing in the end note makes the story less credible. It is a little like a bank teller referring a customer to the president of the same bank in order for the customer to learn whether or not the bank is sound.

Or if someone writes to the organization with the description of an injury that caused severe physical deformity of an ankle, wrist, or other part of the body, then describes a healing through prayer, how does a person verify that the story actually happened? Some members will accept the story based on the fact that they would not lie, so why would anyone else falsify such an incident? Other members want proof but are willing to accept the testimony of the person's friend or family member, again given by letter from what may be a long distance away. And some accept that the injury and healing are possible but would prefer to have documentation from a doctor or other potentially skeptical source. (Remember that traumatic injuries of this type can be set by a doctor without violating the tenets of the faith.) An objective outsider, however, is most likely to say that the story is interesting yet neither proves nor disproves anything because it is only the person's word.

When People Don't Get Better

When Christian Science practices don't work and people stay sick, they are said to be involved in malpractice. The term "malpractice" means that the sick person's mind was under assault by false reasoning, which, when accepted, develops negative powers that can overwhelm all the good work of practitioners and others.

Malpractice can occur in different ways. The most common is by believing false ideas, ideas contrary to Eddy's teachings. It is extremely difficult to cure someone of heart disease if, instead of trusting fully in God and the teachings of Mrs. Eddy, the sufferer thinks, "If my prayers fail to work, I can always undergo surgery"; this person is guilty of malpractice. Another way malpractice can occur is if the ill person does not take precautions to protect himself or herself from the negative thoughts and doubts expressed by other people.

In her own life, the founder of the Christian Science

Church was convinced that it was deliberate malpractice that led to the death of her last husband, Asa Gilbert Eddy. She thought that an early student who had apparently broken with her was using mesmeric poisoning against her husband. Unfortunately the malpractice was so skillful that to someone not knowledgeable about such matters—a pathologist, for example—the death appeared to have been caused by arsenic poisoning. But Mrs. Eddy was convinced that she knew the truth.

Christian Science and Children

Christian Science has come under much criticism over the years because of its teachings regarding health-care practices for the children of its church members. The story of Seth Glaser illustrates one of the problems.

When their seventeen-month-old son, Seth, became ill in March of 1984, Lise and Eliot Dixon Glaser called on the help of Virginia Scott, a Christian Science practitioner. Despite the prayer and counsel of the practitioner, Seth died.[15] Because the circumstances of Seth's death were unusual, the county coroner asked for an investigation of the events surrounding the young boy's death.

The detectives who were assigned to the case found the Glasers to be a loving, sincere couple who had seen Christian Science work and felt it was the best way for their son to be treated. When Lise Glaser was asked what she would tell other Christian Science mothers about her loss, her response was,

> I would say, [Christian Science] works. I know it works. I know [Seth] was blessed by being here with us. . . . See, we feel that Christian Science is helping us get that ultimate goal of just being perfect, okay? And that this experience helped him on his way. Not this experience, this one, but I mean being with us and feeling the love and sharing the love and having the advantage of Christian Science. I see that as an advantage, the advantage of Christian Science treatment and

the growing awareness of some of the laws that are timeless and eternal. They apply here just as much as so called in heaven or before. I would say, I would say it works, and I know it works. And even though we didn't demonstrate it in this instance, you . . . be true to what you feel is the most right thing in any situation. Don't forsake what you've known just because of this. I'd say, "Search out. Make sure you know what you're doing because—you know, if someone isn't as firm as I am, and I'm not as firm as some others, but I am firm, more firm than a lot of people. Then if you're going through a situation where there's going to be any doubt at all, they should go medical."[16]

Regardless of the facts, the law enforcement officers felt that there was a clear case of child endangerment and possible involuntary manslaughter. The parents had felt they were acting in the best interests of their child. They relied on treatments consistent with their religious beliefs, and they unquestionably loved their son. Under normal circumstances, it is possible the couple would have been left alone to grieve. Because this case affected others practicing Christian Science, however, it ultimately went to court, where it was heard before a judge in December of 1989.

The judge refused to put the Church of Christ, Scientist, on trial. Expert medical evidence made it clear that the point when the Glasers would have reason to believe their child was seriously ill, perhaps in crisis, was also a point that was too late to save him. In other words, even if they had taken Seth at that point to the greatest medical facility in the nation, the child still would have died. The Glaser boy simply did not exhibit symptoms the average parent would ever suspect might indicate something more serious than a mild influenza until it was too late for anyone to save him. The case was dismissed.

Other parents have not been so fortunate. While they are not being placed in jail, parents whose children die following the work of Christian Science practitioners rather than medical professionals are being convicted of crimes such as child abuse, child neglect, involuntary manslaughter, or child endangerment. Judges and juries have compassion for the sincerity of the grieving couple. Yet respect for their beliefs does not alter the law.[17]

Christian Scientists offer two explanations of what happened to the Glaser family. One explanation holds that it was simply the child's time to die. All life is finite, and it is God who knows what each person's life will be. For Seth Glaser, seventeen months is what had been allotted, his life serving a purpose only the Creator knows. There is nothing to be upset about when an infant dies within a matter of months of his birth. A second explanation relates to the issue of malpractice. The parents' fear or concern about the child gave the disease power and strength. Others, including non-Christian Scientist family members and friends, may have been worried about the child's illness, again giving the illness ever greater power.

Christian Scientists are instructed to teach their children from infancy that illness does not exist. "Children should be taught the Truthcure, Christian Science, among their first lessons, and kept from discussing or entertaining theories or thoughts about sickness. To prevent the experience of error and its sufferings, keep out of the minds of your children either sinful or diseased thoughts. The latter should be excluded on the same principle as the former. This makes Christian Science early available."[18]

These beliefs put parents in controversial positions with several laws governing health care for children. Most states require mandatory vaccinations of infants and school-aged children. Because this violates the tenets of Christian Science teaching, parents are urged to gain exemptions from such requirements. George Channing clarifies the Christian Science Church's position: "Christian Scientists do not oppose vaccination for those who want it and believe in it.

They do oppose compulsory vaccination for Christian Scientists—as a trespass upon their religious convictions."[19]

In other situations children request exemptions from any degree of health care that requires medicines or invasive procedures or from academic courses they would encounter in school. "The only instruction to which Christian Scientists object is that which tends to set up the method of material medicine as the *only* healing method or system. Christian Scientists object to picturing the process of disease in ways which visualize the terror which begets disease. They also object to compulsory medical regulations because, in effect, such regulations constitute indoctrination which may undermine the religious teaching of the home."[20]

Do children of Christian Scientists have fewer illnesses? Friends of Christian Scientists or teachers of Christian Science children have noticed that such children are sick less frequently than other children. Is this because the children are not sick or because children of practicing Christian Scientists are not going to complain?

Certainly we have no way of knowing. Children, who are young in the faith, would be influenced by the comments and actions of their parents. And they have nothing to gain by talking about any symptoms. They are going to be attending school, social activities, and whatever else might be unpleasant, regardless of how they feel physically. So why should they bother saying they're sick? Neither family nor the Church will accept a declaration of symptoms as being justification for anything other than, when necessary, the use of a practitioner.

While the Christian Science faith remains fairly strong, its membership seems to be on the decline, and the cases involving child deaths are causing new scrutiny of the religion. Memberships are not revealed, and its respected newspaper, *The Christian Science Monitor,* has declined in circulation to 150,000, which includes all or almost all Scientists as well as many outsiders.

More important, some studies are beginning to show that Christian Scientists live a somewhat shorter period of time than other Christians. If such studies are repeatedly verified, they will certainly cast further doubts on the Christian Science teachings.

9

The Merging of the Church and Medicine

During the last four centuries, changes in both the church and science have affected how we view Christian faith and healing today. As we look at the development of both the church and medicine, we see the various threads in the fabric of contemporary faith healing.

DEVELOPMENTS IN THE CHURCH

From the Judaic tradition we have seen the influence of the Old Testament and the rabbinical writings in the Talmud. The perspective of healing in these writings included a mixture of divine intervention, medicine as it was understood in those times, and superstition. The early Christian church followed the teachings of Christ and practiced healing in their worship groups. Centuries later the Roman Catholic Church gained its direction from the popes, who were considered to be infallible. Spiritual direction was given not through reading the Bible or through prayer but through the church hierarchy: the popes instructed the cardinals, who instructed the bishops, who instructed the priests, who instructed the people. The popes' word was law.

In the early 1500s, Martin Luther challenged the church hierarchy and stressed the need to look to the Bible as the source of spiritual authority. As Luther and other reformers broke away from the Catholic Church, the Protestant movement began, with small groups adhering to their separate interpretation of Scripture.

Revivalism

By the middle of the eighteenth century, the ideas of Luther returned to the American colonies in the form of revivalists like George Whitefield. Whitefield, although he was a scholarly theologian, conducted worship services that resembled theater more than the ceremonious assemblies associated with the Christian church before this time. His goal was to communicate with his listeners. Whitefield was a storyteller who used anecdotes to humanize and contemporize biblical teachings. His dramatic oratory involved his audience in whatever he was preaching. If he preached about God's dislike for sin, he made the people feel as if they were nothing more than a pinch of dust held between the fingers of an angry God.

As the eighteenth century ended, the dramatic style of preaching gained a strong audience among the people of the western frontier. The people enjoyed the "show," with the preacher strutting and shouting, making the Bible and faith come alive. They liked the emotional excitement of what came to be considered a revival meeting. They liked being able to shout with joy, recoil with horror, moan, scream, and generally express themselves during services.

Area-wide revival meetings, also called camp meetings, were especially colorful. People who normally lived in isolation, sometimes having to travel for miles to see their nearest neighbors, joined together for singing and worship during the days of the revival meeting. They ate together, talked together, and experienced oratory as colorful as their normal lives were drab.

During the Civil War era, Charles Finney brought the revival meetings of the frontier into the sophisticated world of the cities. The new form of services were quite different from those in the past. Music involved praise lyrics sung to simple popular tunes. Each service included an altar call, a time in which the minister invited members of the audience to come forward to repent of their past, surrender their lives to Christ, and have a new future.

During this era the Bible was seen as the unerring word of God. Each chapter was to be believed in its literal translation. If an idea did not have its source in the Bible, then it wasn't valid.

Emerging Science

Medical science, which had long been a hit-or-miss affair, also gained momentum, even though it was slow. For instance, in the middle of the nineteenth century, a young Viennese doctor named Ignaz Semmelweis noticed that patients often died after they had been examined by a doctor or medical student who had recently done an autopsy. Semmelweis instructed the personnel to wash their hands after each autopsy, resulting in fewer patient deaths. Still later Semmelweis perceived that diseases also were transmitted from living patient to living patient, so he ordered that all medical personnel wash their hands after examining each living patient.

Immediately howls of protest were raised against the "nuisance" of washing, washing, washing—but the mortality rate went down further. Was Semmelweis acclaimed by his fellows? On the contrary, lazy students, prejudiced obstetricians, and jealous superiors scorned and belittled him so much that his annual contract was not renewed. His successor threw out the wash basins and up shot the mortality rate to the old terrifying figures. Were his colleagues convinced? Not at all! . . . Dr. Semmelweis wrote an excellently documented book on his work, which only spurred his assailants to the bitterest sarcasm. The strain plus the death cries of dying mothers so haunted him and weighed on his sensitive nature that his mind finally broke. Ignaz Semmelweis died in a mental institution without ever receiving the recognition he richly deserved.[1]

In an era in which seemingly minor ailments—influenza, measles, diarrhea, and the like—still created plague-like numbers of deaths, safe medical practices gradually were instituted. Doctors learned to isolate people with contagious diseases. Eventually doctors realized Semmelweis' ideas were sound, and they sterilized their hands and all medical instruments. Surgery was being performed under anesthetic.

As the nineteenth century came to a close, new inventions made a major impact on society. Science was beginning to make significant strides. Optical instruments brought a better understanding of the planets, the suns, and outer space. Cars were soon to be developed, and flying machines would soon be a reality. Within a few decades radio and television technology, telephones and moving pictures would change the face of American culture.

Clash of Faith and Science

These new inventions and advances created a crisis of faith for many Christians. They were faced with new questions of how to integrate this scientific knowledge into their faith.

Some people responded by embracing scientific advances as a new god. They saw no conflict between science and faith. In fact many of them questioned the need for God and faith. Maybe the human mind was all that was needed. Given time and study, perhaps men and women could solve all of life's problems.

Other people felt overwhelmed and saw scientific advances as a threat to their faith. Where science had once been taught as a way to glorify God through the study of his creation, this new scientific research seemed to be almost blasphemous. Were scientists trying to be like God? Were they entering a domain reserved only for the Divine?

Many people felt scientists were overreaching human boundaries in bringing radical new gadgets to everyday life. Talking over a wire, illuminating a room by throwing a switch instead of lighting a candle, trying to replace the horse or fly like birds seemed a dangerous affront to the Creator. The sudden changes in people's lives made them fearful of the new, of the scientists, of the secular world. What was sinful? What was the danger in using these new devices?

These questions led many Christians to hold tightly to what they considered to be the fundamentals of the Christian faith and to cling tenaciously to their literal translations of the Bible. These Christians, later to be called fundamentalists, believed that the basic facts everyone needed to know were in the Bible. It was all right to drive cars, to undergo surgery, or to live in a community that was gradually seeing the introduction of electric lights. If a scientific statement seemed to be inconsistent with one of the Bible's truths, however, then the scientific statement was wrong. They said that any statement of history or science made in the Bible was factual.

FAITH, SCIENCE, AND HEALING

How Christians saw the Bible and science affected how they viewed healing. Their distrust of science influenced the various faith-healing movements that established themselves in the first quarter of the twentieth century.

Internationally, the English were ahead of the Americans in developing support for the idea of healing the sick through prayer. The first Divine Healing Conference was held in London in 1885, with delegates from many countries of the world. There was no single theology among the participants. Instead, they shared a longing for renewed involvement of the Holy Spirit in their lives.

The Roman Catholic Church had long held that healing was one of the important gifts of the Spirit. But the church was conservative compared to the practitioners of the newer forms of Protestantism.

The Pentecostal movement became one of the leading proponents of the supernatural element of religion and the manifestation of the Spirit. Pentecostals played off the Holiness movement that preceded them, a nineteenth-century movement that talked of personal holiness through the Holy Spirit. Pentecostals believed that a person had to experience the "baptism in the spirit" in order to be converted. And the way this baptism was revealed was through the speaking in tongues. A "full gospel" Pentecostal believed that Jesus Christ entered lives in three ways—as healer, savior, and baptizer in the Spirit. A Christian needed to accept all three experiences.

The Pentecostal movement spread quickly from its founding in Los Angeles in 1906. The ideas expressed by the Pentecostals, however, seemed to evolve almost simultaneously in different parts of the country. Charles Parham broke from the Methodist church to preach Pentecostalism throughout the Midwest. A. J. Tomlinson formed the

Church of God, drawing converts from North Carolina and eastern Tennessee. Other leaders formed their groups, defining their theology and practice apart from the influence of other groups.

This was not a movement of identical thoughts. Although all Pentecostals shared a belief in the baptism of the Holy Spirit, they were not of one mind. The first break among the Pentecostals came with the issue of organization. Some groups advocated independence and autonomy. Like-minded people would select a leader and form their own church. But other Pentecostals wanted a more structured organization. They wanted churches that could share a common leadership and hierarchical structure of church government.

Then there were doctrinal and social issues. Were the names God, Jesus, and the Holy Spirit actually three different ways of saying the Creator? Or was there a triune leadership of Father, Son, and Holy Spirit? What about the issues of marriage, divorce, and remarriage? And if a church condemned divorce within its membership, how were they to treat a divorced man and divorced woman, each of whom had been led to Jesus through a Pentecostal experience *after* their respective divorces? And what if that man and woman, now seemingly right with the Lord, wanted to marry within their new faith?

The Healing Revival

After World War II, many of the expressions of the Christian church—whether Catholic or Protestant, mainstream, evangelical, or Pentecostal—included healing revivals. Revival preachers traveled from community to community, setting up tents, preaching the Word, perhaps speaking in tongues if they were so inclined, and healing the sick. Preachers' success was advertised by how many people had been healed—50 in one town, 300 in another, 125 in a third, or however many turned out. Record keeping was more of an advertising gimmick than an accurate clinical account of what happened. And few revival preachers remained in any of the towns where they worked their "miracles" to see the long-term results of their actions.

For the public, the healing revivals became either an important aspect of their spiritual growth, bringing them new ways to look at life and faith, or a fascinating show. Many of the healing revivals were held during the summer, offering music, singing, an exciting performer, a chance to shout, dance, and be diverted from the farms and the everyday cares they all faced.

Revival healing was another form of patent medicine for some.[2] It made them feel good, got their mind off their troubles, and if it didn't work, the days or evenings in the tent were still well spent.

And so the mainstream and off-beat religions filled American communities with a wide variety of ideas about healing, ministry, and the proper way to worship God. Attitudes toward healing and health were being formed in all the groups. Some played off the historical teachings of the Old and New Testaments, the Talmud, and other religious writings. Others evolved from biblical interpretations, sometimes taken out of context, sometimes of questionable accuracy. Still others evolved from the acceptance and understanding of the development of the science of medicine with its new discoveries about disease, infection, and trauma.

THE DEVELOPMENTS IN MEDICAL SCIENCE

The evolution of modern science ran a parallel path to the evolving religious philosophies. By today's standards, the concepts seem humorous or dangerously naïve. Still, the idea that surgery could be performed safely, that there were minute life forms that could affect our health, that products could be developed to treat illness, all seemed to empower the human mind in ways never before seen.

By the end of the Civil War, with the nation more keenly aware of the horrors of violent trauma (gunshot wounds, stabbings, deliberately broken bones, etc.) than ever before, medicine became the most respected profession in the nation. Doctors were desired everywhere, especially in parts of the country that had been devastated by battles or the periodic epidemics of smallpox, cholera, diphtheria, typhoid, influenza, and other major killers of the time.

The nature of society and education, however, was such that the profession was still far from what might be expected. Of the over one hundred medical schools in existence at the time, most of them required very little for admission. The elite among them required a high school diploma, but most would settle for someone who was reasonably literate, an ability achieved by seventh or eighth grade. Training was short and not particularly arduous. Except for those students who chose to do clinical or laboratory work, students became doctors in a year's time. Many doctors found that their truly sick patients would die, and there was nothing they could do to help. By 1872, doctors demanded longer training programs and the chance for postgraduate studies. Only a few schools complied.

Until approximately 1875, when medical schools first began to expand their courses, the best trained doctors were those who went through an apprentice program. They would select a doctor they admired, offer him a fee that ranged from $100 to $250 and offer to do other labor like chopping wood and running errands in exchange for assisting the doctor and learning from him. During the course of three years, the apprentice would read books about biology, anatomy, and similar subjects, asking the doctor questions as he learned. He would accompany the doctor on his practice, learning what would today be considered basic first aid. From there he would graduate to assisting with surgeries, administering bleedings, helping with amputations, and learning whatever else the doctor did in his practice.[3]

Physicians in those days probably caused as much ill health as they cured. Their tools were primitive, and such basic items as stethoscopes and thermometers, although in existence, were not widely used before 1880. There were no masks or gowns used for surgery, and misconceptions, such as the idea that the bleeding of a patient was beneficial, often caused serious shock and death.

The success of a medical practice was not necessarily based on the competence of the physician. In some communities, the politics of the doctor determined his patient list. For example, if a town was predominantly Republican and the doctors were mostly Democrats, there would be a physician shortage in the community. The Republicans would usually not patronize the Democrat physicians. It was an odd situation, but given the state of medical care, it seems that the people did as well whether they saw a physician or used home remedies.

Doctors earned little money in their practices. They worked seven days a week (a "light" practice usually allowed for a half day Sunday to one's self), maintained office hours primarily for transients, and regularly had to make house calls. They traveled by horse and buggy, allowing for only limited sleep. Even worse, pay was often in barter. One patient might supply a quantity of apple brandy in exchange for an operation, another offering chickens, bushels of corn, or similar items. It was even worse for country doctors, who were considered a friend within the community, and that meant doing some of their work either without charge or at a greatly reduced price because of their patient's limited circumstances.

Larger amounts of money often came from pharmaceuticals. Physicians tried to limit their patients' use of patent medicines—potions and remedies sold by peddlers or town merchants. Some doctors formed their own drug stores, making their own prescriptions and profiting from the sideline. Other doctors asked the pharmacists to encourage patients to use the doctor and whatever passed for "real" medicine at the time instead of the patent cures. In exchange for the business, the doctor would kick back a percentage to the pharmacist, both of them profiting.

The hostility toward patent medicines, which reached their zenith of popularity toward the end of the nineteenth century, was based on outrageous claims having no basis in truth. Sometimes the manufacturers invented diseases to be cured. These included "brain fatigue, the female complaint, and torpid liver," among many others. Other times the treatments were used for illnesses that could not be treated by conventional medicine. And still other ads described products "essential" to good health, like the "Universal" Coffee Percolator offered in this ad:

> The people who drink boiled coffee . . . are slowly *tanning* their stomachs! For *boiled* coffee contains the same biting acid that Tanners use to make leather out of cowhides . . . And just as Tannin eats the flesh out of cowhides, so does it—when extracted in boiling coffee—destroy the tender mucous lining of the throat, stomach and intestines.
>
> That's why drinkers of *boiled* coffee nearly always suffer from dyspepsia—why they are extremely nervous and irritable.
>
> Now, isn't there some way in which Coffee can be made that will eliminate the injurious Tannin and give only the Good Elements that are healthful?
>
> Yes . . . there is a way—*one way only*—of getting rid of the Bad in Coffee and obtaining only the Good, and that's by using the "Universal" Coffee Percolator.

Popular patent medicines included Dr. Clarke's Home Treatment, the perfect cure for obesity (causing no wrinkles or flabbiness); Colethia to cure extreme leanness, making the user healthfully plump; Blair's Pills for Gout and Rheumatism; and McIlhenny's Tabasco Sauce for an aid to digestion. Dr. Wilson's Electric Belt For Ladies claimed to be a treatment for malaria, back pain, abdominal troubles, female weakness, liver and kidney disease, and a host of other serious ailments. Other patent medicines, some harmless, some containing ingredients that could be addictive or dangerous, included Ginger Tonic, Ayer's Pills and Ayer's Cherry Pectoral, Watson's Neuralgia King, and even Allcock's Porous Plasters, which helped everything from malaria to rheumatism and kidney disorders. Most contained alcohol to one degree or another. Some compounds, however, contained opium, chloroform, cocaine, morphine, and similar drugs.

Shortly before the turn of the century, the understanding of illness increased tremendously. Physicians had begun the specialty of pathology, where they were able to observe the causes of death through analysis of body organs and tissues. This was an advance that helped them relate patients' symptoms with what eventually happened to them. In addition, doctors had developed the awareness of germs as a cause of disease. Yet even though the causes were understood, yellow fever, influenza, tuberculosis, and similar diseases destroyed large segments of the population. Doctors could do little to fight them.

The arrival of the family doctor was a little like the arrival of a faith healer. Part of the aid to the patient came from the presence of the physician. The person was sick, and when a caring man or woman came to the home, medical bag in hand, the emotional reaction was extremely positive. There was a placebo effect that even the physicians of the day admitted existed.

Diagnosis of illness was relatively simple, and the black bag the physicians carried implied there were all manner of cures. In truth, if the patient were suffering from insomnia or from pain that kept the person awake, the doctor would provide chloral hydrate (knock-out drops). Other drugs included barbiturates for high blood pressure, nitroglycerine to ease the pain of angina, and what was then a universal pain killer—morphine. The latter was highly addictive, but in those instances where the patient was given too much, the numbing effect resulted in the individual simply not caring.

Because traditional medicine offered so much knowledge about the symptoms of illness and so little about its treatment, nontraditional "professionals" became popular. Some put together various herbs and plants in teas and other forms that had some healing properties, much as Native Americans had done with plants for generations. In other instances, the combinations were meaningless or could even cause a violent allergic reaction that would lead to more serious illness or death.

There were water cures, enema cures, and numerous other treatments. Each had well-trained practitioners, though often they were well trained in fields that offered no relief whatever. In fact, it was not until 1915 that serious professionals began to look for the licensing and specialization of medical treatment. They tried to limit care to dentists, pharmacists, surgeons, optometrists, and the like, eliminating the obvious quacks, though what today would be considered medical malpractice was frequently a part of early treatment.

Hospital care was also of limited value during this period. The hospitals were long-term facilities in which hygiene was such that many patients became worse from the experience, often entering for a serious though seemingly non-life-threatening problem, then dying after a month or more of care. The fact that even four weeks in the hospital was considered a fairly short stay added to the risks patients encountered.

Poor sanitation practices added to the spread of disease. For example, refrigerators (ice boxes) had drain pipes for the melting water, but these pipes were connected to other house drains through which waste products were dumped. Feces, urine, spoiled food, and other dangerous items were thus directly linked to the cold storage area for food. Toilets existed, but the inability to have adequate water pressure meant that flushing was not always possible. Sometimes fecal material would stay in what was little more than a sophisticated slop bucket for several hours before a servant would hand pour water to compensate for the lack of pressure. Even furnaces were not designed to protect the homes from breathing fouled air. In fact, after President James A. Garfield died, physicians examining conditions in the White House concluded that he might have survived had the plumbing and food storage areas been more sanitary.

FURTHER MERGING AND CLASH OF FAITH AND SCIENCE

The knowledge of medicine forced major changes in how people viewed faith and healing. Conflicts and compromises were developing as never before. The knowledge and beliefs of the late nineteenth and early twentieth centuries would set the stage for the time when science would make its greatest advances in all of recorded history.

In the 1960s, heart transplants became a reality. Suddenly thoracic (chest) surgeons became the new heroes. They were the controllers of life. They could transport a piece of a dead person (the still-beating heart) and place it in the dying in order to restore the living. Even Jesus had done nothing so miraculous in the eyes of many. The American news and picture magazines fêted these pioneers, making names such as Cooley, DeBakey, and Jarvik household words.

Many Americans began looking at science in one of two ways—either as a replacement for religion or as a field that had to be "bettered" by religious leaders. Can a physician cure cancer through surgery? Then a faith healer must cure it by the laying on of hands, by prayer, or by pronouncing a healing in the name of Jesus. Either there was no all-powerful God (a God of limited action might be all right, though certainly a disappointment in a crisis) or God had to put on a magic show to be believable. The idea that humans could grow in their knowledge of existence, could develop conveniences, could learn to cure some diseases, create inventions to fly through the air or swim under water and still be a people of God was confusing at best.

The fundamentalist movement had a great deal of difficulty with the new advances. If the Bible did not record the existence of airplanes, then is it right for humans to try to fly? If the Bible did not speak of computers, automobiles, radios, or televisions, then did any of these advances have a place in the lives of Christians? If the Bible is the unerring word of God, if we are to live exactly according to the words in the Bible, then how do we handle those scientific creations never mentioned? Are doctors men and women without faith? After all, neither Jesus, nor Luke, the physician, nor the other disciples ever healed through surgery or medication given by injection. If the doctors have to use invasive techniques to heal, does this make them lacking in faith at best, sacrilegious at worst?

These questions, changes, new understandings, and clashes shaped the faith-healing movements in the early part of the twentieth century. The explosion of medical advances continues to challenge our thinking in the rest of the twentieth century, as the next chapter will reveal.

III
Conclusions

10

Health and Wholeness

As we approach the beginning of the twenty-first century, medical understanding, research, practice, and technology have reached a level of unprecedented sophistication. While that should give us great encouragement and hope, we should not allow these advances to lull us into a complacency or an expectation that illness will be eradicated. As long as humans live on this earth, we will face disease—and we will need healing.

As we look for healing in our own lives, let's be sure that we look in the right places. These final chapters will focus on two issues: first, our personal responsibility in maintaining health; and second, gaining discernment as we seek healing through God's power.

OUR MIRACULOUS BODIES

God has created within each of our bodies miraculous healing forces. Our intricate immune system constantly monitors our body's cellular health. And when its sensors detect a threat, the immune system immediately sends out warrior cells to combat the threat. All of this goes on without a single conscious thought on our part.

Good health is the intended state of the human body, and every aspect of our existence is a fight to maintain or return to this condition. Cut your finger and it starts to bleed, creating the risk of death through loss of blood or external infection entering your body. Then the blood clots, the flow is stanched, a scab forms, and new skin is made to eliminate any trace of the original cut and to end the risks to which you had been exposed. It is an experience you will have thousands of times during your life because it is one of the ways our Creator has assured our survival.

Break a bone in your leg, and you won't be able to walk properly. You won't be able to support your own weight. You'll hop about, use crutches, or sit in a wheelchair. But almost as soon as your bone breaks, it starts to heal. If you, a first-aid expert, a doctor, or someone else is able to push the broken bone back into position, then immobilize it enough so it heals in that position, you'll be fine. In a matter of weeks the bone will be as strong as ever.

Be beaten, battered, and told you are rotten as a child, and you will be emotionally in ruins, filled with anger, self-hate, and self-doubt. Yet through talking with others, through self-help programs, therapy, and any number of other options, you can discover that you do have value, that you are worth loving. You achieve emotional healing, no longer a victim of your past.

Eat the wrong foods and you will find yourself craving certain vegetables, salads, fruit, and other essential nourishment. Drink too little liquid and you will crave water. Again your body's healing mechanisms are trying to function despite your attempts to ignore what is needed for good health.

Get too little sleep and your body will make you rest. You suddenly find you have to "crash," to take a nap, to restore yourself.

Even the best of surgeons do not heal us. They simply restructure the body so that it functions as it should have done, or they remove a tumor that is abnormal. They correct what has gone wrong. They do not create wellness; they try to help you put your body in the best position for your God-given healing forces to do their job.

Even medication is used as a means for returning the body to its natural state. Pain killers are meant to ease suffering while the body heals itself. Drugs to stop diarrhea or vomiting are meant to stop unnatural conditions while the body heals. Even pharmaceuticals used to correct problems with the thyroid, with growth, or insulin, among others, are meant only to restore the body to its intended function.

TAKE RESPONSIBILITY

God is the healer, and he heals in miraculous and mysterious ways. And we may look to him for healing. But we must never overlook the responsibility he has given each of us to keep our bodies in the best possible condition for their natural healing forces to work. As we said in earlier chapters, we can't ignore good health practices or abuse our bodies and then expect God to heal us and rescue us from our own decisions.

The Importance of Community

We must live and act in community to achieve and maintain the greatest possible physical, emotional, and spiritual health. Studies have shown that group support reduces tension, giving a greater sense of self-worth, of belonging, of having purpose.

The kind of people you associate with also affects your health. Positive, hopeful, life-giving people will encourage health in you. In the same way, angry, bitter, blaming people will create stress in your life, robbing you of health and wholeness. The writer of Proverbs warns, "Do not make friends with a hot-tempered [person], do not associate with one easily angered, or you may learn [that person's] ways and get yourself ensnared" (Prov. 22:24–25).

Studies of ethnic groups whose ways of living have changed over the years reinforce the importance of community even when separated from religion. Japanese and Japanese-Americans who adhere to the tradition of close community ties have an extremely low rate of stress-related ailments, including cancer. This is true regardless of diet and other habits, including smoking. When these same people become Westernized, however, limiting or eliminating those close ties, the rate of heart disease and similar ailments rises sharply. This was true even when diet and other aspects of traditional culture have been retained. Loners who isolate themselves from the community are always at greater risk than people who retain that sense of community, no matter how else they may change their lifestyles.[1]

In the 1950s, studies of workers in rubber, steel, and automobile factories of Detroit, Cleveland, Akron, and Pittsburgh showed that the average worker died within three years of retiring. But if the retired worker found close relationships in clubs, volunteer work, a new job, or some other method of interacting closely with caring people who share the same interests, the retired person's life span was greatly improved. Since all other factors were the same, the conclusion was reached that the person who remains involved in the community will have better health.[2]

Another study also showed that intimacy results in lowered health risks. Married couples, as well as widows, widowers, divorced, and single people in close friendships are at a reduced risk of disease.[3]

The exact reason for health being greater in community is not known. Several theories have evolved, however, all of them probably contributing in one way or another.

First, people in community have a stronger will to live. During an interview with a newly married eighty-year-old former widower who survived an emergency quadruple bypass surgery, I sensed his strong will to live. The nature of his condition had been such that his doctors knew he would be dead in a matter of weeks without the surgery. Yet they also knew that many of their elderly patients had difficulty rallying and healing after the massive surgery. When they discussed the risks with the man, he said he wished to go through with the surgery.

The man recovered in an amazingly short period of time, according to the doctors. The man was up and around in the time they would have expected for someone twenty to thirty years younger. When I talked with the man, he said, "I was so tired after the surgery, I knew I could let myself die. All I had to do was give in to the exhaustion, to not fight."

The man then spoke of his new bride. She had been widowed after almost fifty years in a relationship with a man whom she did not love. His wife's late husband had been self-centered, uncaring, and seemingly unloving. Yet she had believed in the sacredness of marriage, had never strayed, and had never considered a divorce.

Ironically, the heart-surgery patient had come from a similar background, his late wife very much like his new bride's former husband. And he had shared the integrity of his new bride in refusing to cheat or consider divorce an option. The newly married couple had slowly learned to trust each other, and then they had both discovered all the passion, tenderness, and respect they had failed to achieve in their first marriages.

"She told me she wanted me, needed me," the elderly patient said, smiling happily. "No one ever said that to me before, not my late wife, not my children. I knew I could die, but I chose to live. I wasn't afraid of death. I just wanted the pleasure in life I had never experienced before. I wanted to live for her."

The story proved typical of many I would later hear among elderly couples enjoying a strong relationship. They did not always have fewer illnesses than others their own age, but their recovery was often quicker. Sometimes they were enjoying a new relationship following widowhood or divorce. At other times they were enjoying a relationship that had grown ever stronger with the years. Whatever the case, it was for the love of the spouse that they fought for their health, not from a fear of death.

Other studies have revealed that close friendships serve the same functions as a good marriage, though for different reasons. This is why some single people have long lives and others seem to die from ailments from which most men and women their age, with similar health histories, recover.

Several years ago, two psychiatrists at the University of Washington School of Medicine in Seattle put together a scale that rated stress in one's life. The greatest devastation came with the death of a spouse, followed by divorce and marital separation. The least stressful experience rated was a minor violation of the law.

When the scale was first released in the *Journal of Psychosomatic Research,* it was frequently quoted throughout the country. When people who read it added up their stress factors, they became aware of changes they needed to make.

Some combinations of stress seemed to mean a death sentence when they occurred within a twelve-month period. For example, a seventy-two-year-old man who retires, moves from New York to Arizona, changes churches from one where he was on the vestry to one where he is just a part of the congregation, and goes on a diet to become more fit, then has his wife get sick and die, might have a stress-factor score of 306—an almost certain death sentence for a man his age. Later stress studies revealed, however, that if someone undergoing similar life experiences had close friends who were at hand, helping, listening, genuinely caring and accepting, the person would probably survive. Even if the person became ill or suffered fairly long-term depression, with the active support of those friends, healing and a return to good health generally would occur over a period of from one to two years.[4]

The Healing Value of Loving Friendships

The writer of Proverbs wisely describes that relationships with loving people will lead to health: "Reckless words pierce like a sword, but the tongue of the wise brings healing" (Prov. 12:18). Friends who want what is good for us will counsel us in wisdom. They will guide us into practices and attitudes that will lead to health and wholeness.

Psychiatrists and psychologists have long learned that emotional healing comes through talking out problems. Ancient cultures used paid listeners to serve this purpose. A person who was troubled would give a coin to a professional listener, then be able to discuss problems and feelings with a dispassionate stranger. Today good friends and counselors fill this need.

Longtime friends and close family members reminiscing about the past can reduce stress for the ill. There is comfort in the memory of happy times, moments of memory that bring laughter and pleasure. Researchers like Paul Horton, M.D., a psychiatrist and author of *Solace: The Missing Dimension in Psychiatry,* refer to such times as "solacing." He believes that from the time of their birth, all humans develop a special relationship with their mothers. This expands as we get older, spreading to school friends and neighbors, then gradually broadening with our life experiences.

Dr. Horton feels that the teenage years of seeming alienation and rebellion are actually a period of desperate searching for solace. There is the natural early separation from parents, of course, as well as adolescent "angst" that causes many teens to feel they are unique in attitudes, beliefs, and the way others see them. But the real problem teens face, according to Dr. Horton, is the need to find a way for solace.

Children naturally achieve solace through "things"— beloved objects such as stuffed animals, a favorite doll, blankets, and the like. Often a ritual includes a toy, perhaps a special blanket, and even a body position that is "safe" from whatever night fantasies a child may have. Night after night the child gets into bed, perhaps holds or surrounds himself or herself with certain toys, shifts into a special position, and immediately relaxes. All is well. All is peaceful. A comforting sleep can be achieved.

Teenagers are embarrassed by actions that provide solace. They are too adult to curl up with a favorite stuffed animal, yet they don't have the intimate friendships that will allow them to gain solace through companions. They have seldom learned constructive techniques to relax, so many of them involve themselves with overwhelmingly loud music, drugs, and alcohol to try to find a new method for achieving solace.

Dr. Horton's studies confirm what has been learned about pet ownership as well. While animals do not have the same healing powers as a community of friends, family, or a loving spouse, the loving interaction with a pet provides both emotional and physical benefits. This is most obviously seen in more rural areas. Parents whose lifestyles allow their teenage children either to own or have a part-time job where they are involved with horses talk about how happy their teenagers become. The time spent touching, grooming, and talking with the animal calms their emotions and seems to bring them the solace to which Dr. Horton refers. This occurs with more commonly owned animals as well, though because caring for horses is more time consuming, the change is more observable.[5]

But pets provide far more health benefits than simple solace. The University of Pennsylvania wanted to research what happened to patients who had heart attacks, then involved themselves with pets. A report by Alan Beck, Sc.D., and Aaron Katcher, M.D., found that one in five individuals with severe heart disease and no pets would die from that heart disease. When someone owned any sort of enjoyable pet, including something so simple as goldfish they could only watch through a bowl or in an aquarium, the risk of dying was decreased by three percent. Put into a different perspective, approximately 30,000 fewer people will die if they are interacting with a dog, cat, bird, fish, or any other pet.[6]

Ironically, the hospice movement (a network that cares for the dying) illustrates the healing power of understanding relationships. The idea behind the hospice movement is to allow people to die in dignity, comfort, and love, whether or not they had friends or caring relatives in the community. Most of the early facilities were connected with religious groups or had clergy on staff, helping the people find peace with God and themselves as they moved toward death. When the person was alone, the staff acted as family, closely interacting rather than treating the people with the far more limited attention of hospitals and nursing homes. When there were family and friends visiting regularly or staying with the person who was dying, the hospice staff helped those people make peace as well. They helped them cope with the anger, the sadness, the fear of loneliness, and the other emotions everyone experiences when losing a loved one. While the loving care of the hospice workers does not heal the dying patient, it does provide inner healing and peace. Studies of hospice care reveal that patients with terminal ailments lived longer, more comfortably, and with greater happiness than those who died from the same conditions but without close relationships.

Watch What You Eat

Another factor that contributes to health and healing is what we eat. Nutrition has been a factor in health from the beginning of human life. The story of the Garden of Eden is the story of a vegetarian existence, where all that grew, with the exception of the forbidden fruit, was to be cultivated and enjoyed by man and woman. After the flood, the Bible makes clear that the descendants of Noah were allowed to eat most meat and fish. Yet clearly the range of fruits, vegetables, and grains, along with fish, fowl, and meat, are all critical for health. As we have come to understand the human body, we have also come to understand how metabolism occurs, what affects our lives, and which illnesses are related to poor nutrition.

And all of the ideas about nutrition have not been healthy ones. As recently as the 1940s it was believed that everyone should daily consume a certain amount of "empty calories"—pies, cakes, cookies, and other sweets that contained many nutritionally incomplete ingredients. For example, once sugar cane is processed into molasses, refined sugar, or any other form, our bodies need B-complex vitamins to process it. These can come from vitamins stored in the body or through supplements. If taken from supplements, most people have no problems with such foods. We now understand, however, that if these vitamins are taken from the body, they often come from the heart, which is slightly weakened by the loss. Thus the organ is endangered by any diet that contains a large amount of sweets.

In the 1960s some people decided to try macrobiotic diets, consuming large amounts of brown rice and no form of animal or fish protein. Again serious health problems resulted as nutrition experts discovered that the human body requires the type of protein that comes from beef, poultry, and fish. Someone who wanted to follow a vegetarian diet needed to learn the relative amounts and types of protein available from beans since no single bean, such as soy, had full protein that matched what the human body needed for proper nutrition. Only in combination with these animal proteins could beans effectively meet the protein needs of someone following a vegetarian diet.

We continue to make new discoveries. For example, adults need to have a very low level of fat in their diets. Lean red meat may not be as healthy as poultry, but it is far healthier than red meat marbled with fat, such as prime rib. Likewise, nonfat milk is healthful in moderation, especially for women who need the source of calcium even more than men. Children, however, are quite different. While they also should not be eating fatty red meat, they need a higher amount of fat than adults. Whole milk may be better for them than skim milk, for example, at least during certain growth periods. Thus certain ages and stages of life require different foods.

Research has also indicated that certain diseases can be controlled through diet rather than medication. Many forms of hypoglycemia, diabetes, arthritis, and other ailments are now controlled by diet, usually accompanied by a change in exercise.

Knowledge of amino acids, minerals, and the other "building blocks" of food have helped bring new ways to handle common problems. Instead of taking a diet pill as an appetite suppressant, a small amount (a few cubes) of turkey can do the same thing when eaten an hour before a meal. Warmed milk releases a natural calmative. Women who react adversely to milk can add calcium-rich foods such as broccoli to their diet either to stave off or to reduce the problems of osteoporosis. We have learned that the deep fat frying of most fast food restaurants is unhealthy, and several chains have changed or broadened their menus to allow for better choices.

Choose Life

The survival instinct is an inherent part of the human condition. When confronted with danger, our bodies naturally create an adrenaline rush that begins what is called a fight-or-flight reaction. We are prepared either to fight with greater strength than we normally require or to flee as rapidly as our bodies are capable of retreating. This is what makes all the more remarkable the situation when someone deliberately enters a dangerous situation to save another. The courageous acts of fire fighters who rush into burning buildings to save the lives of strangers go against our bodies' natural desire to survive. The same is true for the people who race into speeding traffic to try to move a person from the path of an oncoming car or for the medics who run onto the battlefield to treat a fallen soldier, then drag the person to safety.

Health-care workers have seen people who are so ill that they are bedridden most of each day, continually exhausted, each breath a struggle to achieve. But despite this, one day the ill people seem to push themselves a little harder, staying out of bed a little longer, perhaps, or taking a few steps more each day than they were capable of doing the previous morning. Whatever it is, there is an obvious change, a spark that causes them to heal gradually. They have chosen life.

Studies found in medical and psychological journals repeatedly show that the mind is perhaps the most important factor in healing. For example, in the 1960s an accountant for one of the auto-parts manufacturers in Michigan had a routine physical. The doctor informed him that his work days were over right then. His heart was so bad, he was to never return to the office. He was officially retired, a fact made somewhat easier by his being eligible for extensive lifetime benefits from his company. The doctor was more enlightened than many of that era, however. Instead of creating a cardiac cripple, he told the patient to walk briskly each day, no matter what.

The man was shocked by the diagnosis, yet determined to enjoy the rest of his life. Friends thought the doctor's advice was destructive and told the man the exercise would kill him.

The man did more than start walking, however. He went on a boat he loved. He went fishing. And he and his wife began traveling anywhere they could afford, for as long as they could be away. He never missed a day of walking, and he filled his days with activities he loved.

The man died, of course. And it was a heart attack that killed him—twenty-five years after he was told to stop work "or else." He had chosen to work toward life.

Studies have shown that had the man been frightened of his heart attack, he might have avoided the daily walks that sustained him. Certainly there was a risk from the exertion, but there was a greater risk from not taking such action.

It is critical for the ill person to feel that healing is possible. This requires many things, including faith in God, a willingness to take whatever actions are positive, and an understanding of what healing can be.

Someone who has a bad heart may be saved through prayer. There may be a miraculous restoration. Unexplained healings of this type have been discussed in medical literature for generations, though they are extremely rare. Still, the person must recognize that healing requires more than prayer and the hope that the person will be somehow specially selected by God.

The same is true with diabetes, cancer, withered limbs, and anything else. Most theologians feel it is arrogant to rely solely on God and cruel to say to someone who has been through a faith healing that a relapse or lack of detectable change when tested by a physician is the result of personal sin or other failing. They feel that we must use all of our gifts from God, all of our understanding of his world. This means believing in prayer but also in the healing qualities he has placed within us all. We must be willing to eat correctly, increase our activity in ways that are helpful, use those aspects of medical science that have been shown to work, and generally embrace the future with a positive attitude.

Within my own family, generation after generation on my father's side died from diabetes. Several factors in their lives made diabetes inevitable: high-sugar diet, obesity, and little exercise. When my father's diabetes was diagnosed at the time he was fifty, the doctor told him it had been caused by an improper diet, high in sugar. He was told that he would have to begin taking insulin, but that if he changed his diet, the insulin use would be only temporary. A diet free from sugar would enable him to control the diabetes. With the sugar in his diet, even the insulin might not be able to prevent a slow deterioration of his health.

My father was on insulin a very short period of time. My mother learned how to sweeten without sugar, using such foods as chopped carrots and the liquid skimmed from raisins soaked in water for a day, among other natural sweeteners. For the next thirty-five years, until his death in his mid-eighties, my father controlled his diabetes by eating correctly and taking a walk each day. His parents, his grandparents, and many other of his ancestors never reached their sixtieth birthdays, all of them dying from the disease they refused to control through diet. My father had a positive attitude and chose life.

Those who take a passive role in their health, or those whose attitudes are negative, stand a good chance of dying. Their future hopes for life are not good.

Let Go of Anger

Another step toward health and healing is letting go of the natural anger that you feel about your condition. A person condemned to a wheelchair after an auto accident in which someone else was at fault may harbor great hatred for the driver, for God, and for anyone else he or she feels is responsible. The person may dwell on past abilities instead of living positively with present realities.

Someone blinded at birth because he or she was in an incubator where too much oxygen was used, once a common problem, may curse the medical profession and even others who are sighted. Again, the anger holds the person back.

Adult children of alcoholics, adults who were abuse victims, and others whose past is filled with cruelty and tragedy need to work through their anger and move on in their lives. As they work through their pain in the safety of a support group, they come to accept the past, to refuse to let their pain control their existence, and to accept themselves as valuable human beings. These positive steps allow them to come to the point of forgiveness.

Forgiveness involves not only forgiving the people who acted wrongly but also forgiving one's self for being victimized by preconceived notions. Sometimes this means recognizing that past actions were based on misunderstandings of what took place. At other times it means recognizing the motives of the people who caused the pain. Letting go of anger and coming to a point of acceptance and forgiveness brings health and healing.

For example, Emily (not her real name) was an extremely depressed college student in constant ill health. She experienced a seemingly endless series of colds, flu, and even repeat bouts of pneumonia. She did not care about her condition, did not care if she lived or died. She had no sense of purpose in life, though she was a musician training to become a teacher and highly respected by all her professors.

When Emily was eight years old, she had been molested by her fourteen-year-old half-brother. Not knowing the implication of her actions, she had encouraged his touching until she learned about incest in a health education class in her junior high school. Horrified by what she learned, she told her half-brother they had to stop. Instead of respecting her request, he raped her several times over the following few weeks before moving away from the home. Emily did not report what had happened because she was certain she had caused it.

In therapy, Emily and the therapist discussed what life had been like for her. She had been an unexpected and unwanted baby, whose presence was resented by both her parents. Her mother often had told her how ugly she was. Her mother wanted nothing to do with her, though Emily did everything she could to win approval.

Emily's father was cold to her, though loving to his son (Emily's half-brother) by a previous marriage. The son was the favorite child, and Emily hated him for the love he received, the very love she so desperately wanted.

When Emily's half-brother touched her inappropriately, she disliked it, but she reasoned that if her half-brother was her father's favorite child, then maybe the attention he gave her made her loved as well. She took pride in the fact that she was the special girl to the special child of the father whose love she so desired.

An adult would find such a situation reprehensible; the child was encouraging a taboo act. Yet in the mind of that child, with the limits of her awareness about all aspects of life, this was nothing more than a pleasurable experience. It was only when she became sexually mature and learned the meaning of incest that she was ashamed. She told her half-brother the truth of what they were doing, something she did not realize he had known all along. When he raped her instead, she felt she had brought the violence onto herself. She so hated herself that she refused to embrace life. In theory, had the repeated illnesses continued, she ultimately would have died.

In therapy, Emily learned to look at the situation through the eyes of that lonely, hurting child. She came to forgive her brother, whom she realized was driven by his own anger and pain in life, and to forgive herself. She joined a support group and moved forward in life, respecting who she was, knowing that God loved her for her present actions, no matter what had happened in her past. Then, within a matter of weeks, her health improved. The illnesses that had plagued her since her junior-high years no longer troubled her.

Take an Active Role

Dr. Bernard Siegel, a surgeon who has been extensively involved with the psychology of illness, frequently talks about self-induced healing. This concept evolved from working with cancer patients and others with life-threatening ailments. It also came from his education in workshops such as the ones conducted at the Simonton Cancer Counseling Center in Texas, where many terminally ill patients have learned to change their attitudes toward life and illness, to become positive about living rather than adjusting to dying.[7]

Dr. Siegel discovered that one of the keys to getting well despite a supposedly terminal illness is a willingness to take part in the recovery process. The patients had to learn to change their lifestyles, yet when they did, in a statistically improbable number of cases, they did not die.

But such a situation is not normal within our society, as Dr. Siegel discovered. After he learned how to help his patients more effectively learn to live despite having a supposedly incurable problem, he contacted one hundred patients he thought could learn to get well or prolong the quality of their lives. He offered these patients, all of whom had cancer that eventually should have been terminal, a chance to come to group therapy sessions to learn a better way to live. Only twelve showed up. The rest were seemingly content to let the cancer destroy them.

Over the years, Dr. Siegel made the discovery that no one needs to give up control to illness. Everyone can benefit from a change of lifestyle, and many of the people who make that change lead long, rich lives that supposedly were "impossible."

Siegel discovered the importance of the patient's attitude toward the illness. He found a predictable breakdown of attitudes. Approximately twenty percent of all patients have lives in such turmoil that they embrace death, whether or not they admit that this is what they are doing. Another sixty percent look on the doctor as the expert on their health. Instead of recognizing that no one knows more about their bodies than they do, and that no one has the stake in their getting well that they have, they view illness the way they might a broken water pipe, a leaking roof, or a problem with electrical wiring: they call the specialist. They go to the doctor, whom they assume will prescribe drugs, order surgery, or some other form of therapy. They follow the orders, do what is necessary, and if it doesn't seem to work, then they decide they did the best they could. The problem is that these people feel relatively helpless without that doctor to guide them.

And the remaining twenty percent of patients demand to take charge of their lives and their health. They redirect their lives. They work both with and apart from medical professionals. They avail themselves of whatever is necessary to get well and to endure the trauma of the illness, including group sharing sessions, psychological counseling, diet, exercise, or anything else.

What prevents people from participating in the healing their bodies could experience? My experience with arthritis and my doctor provide some clues. When I went to Dr. John Holbrook, an internist specializing in arthritis treatment and research, to discuss the chronic degenerative rheumatoid arthritis that severely affected the joints of my hand, we discussed treatment, but we also discussed lifestyle and family history. He learned that childhood emotional problems were physically manifested in ways that caused severe nutritional deficiencies, primarily with vitamin C and the B-complex vitamins. Since these deficiencies are precursors of rheumatoid arthritis (there are many conditions and circumstances that can cause it, my circumstances being one of them), I asked what would happen if I changed what I did and what I ate.

Without going into the details, Dr. Holbrook worked with me on a program that changed many of my habits. I took long, rapid walks each day to improve my cardiovascular condition. I used a heating pad to bake each hand every night for whatever period of time was required to ease the discomfort, planning on reading or watching television during that otherwise boring period. And my diet was altered to address what appeared to have been the original cause of the deterioration.

Over a five-year period, I worked with Dr. Holbrook, periodically using drugs or aspirin and having my blood checked on a regular basis. But by the time we were done, although the joint damage that existed will never be repaired, my blood tests revealed a remarkable reversal. Had the plan not worked, I would have had my finger joints surgically replaced with artificial ones.

I asked the doctor why more people didn't use the recent understanding of the origins and treatments of arthritis rather than relying solely on drugs to ease the symptoms. Many of the drugs routinely prescribed for arthritis have serious side effects, like eyesight deterioration and depression.

The doctor explained that physicians run a risk of being unfairly accused of malpractice if they don't meet the patient's requests. A patient who wants pain stopped isn't going to be satisfied with a doctor who says that the pain should be endured during the healing process when another physician, seemingly equally competent, instantly prescribes a drug to mask the symptom. The patients demand the instant cures and become irate when they are not provided.

Disbelieving what I had been told, I telephoned attorneys specializing in medical malpractice cases. They explained that they did not go to court for frivolous cases. They could not afford to sue a doctor unless the case was such that the jury could legitimately award the victim at least $100,000. "People are convinced that a doctor's job is to eliminate their pain and suffering," said a New York attorney. "They're too lazy and stupid to let the doctor cure them. I had one obese woman in her fifties who wanted to sue her doctor for telling her he wouldn't treat her diabetes unless she went on a diet and started eating properly. He told her that he couldn't keep giving her medicine while she lived on candy and cookies that were killing her. He wasn't helping her. He was just delaying the inevitable.

"She couldn't take hearing that. I don't know if she wanted to be sick, wanted the attention, or just wouldn't believe that she could die. But she did want to sue that man. And that was for his being an honest physician about what was wrong with her and what she could be doing about it."

Other attorneys made similar comments. People want a magic pill because it's easier than enduring a long and sometimes painful treatment that ultimately will make them well.

God can instantly cure diabetes. But if the person who has been afflicted returns to a high-sugar diet, refuses to become active, and otherwise acts self-destructively, the condition is almost certain to return. By contrast, when prayer, medicine, nutrition, exercise, and an effort to maintain a strong sense of self are all combined, long- and short-term healing can take place. The body can take far more abuse than it should. But continued abuse following the discovery of a problem, such as an extremely obese person refusing to lose weight after a heart attack, is challenging God's creation in a way that will not allow for healing.

WHOLENESS

Healing must also be looked on in a broader way than just the miraculous change in someone's body. For example, Mary Verdi-Fletcher is a nationally prominent modern dancer, the founder of her own professional company, and an associate of the internationally known Cleveland Ballet. She teaches, conducts workshops for dancers, and gives demonstrations of dance to schools, clubs, and organizations in a multi-state region. Her performances are lauded by experts in dance, and she has been declared a "natural" by all who have seen her.

Yet Mary Verdi-Fletcher has not been able to walk since she was ten years old. Her legs are short, shattered, useless. She performs from a wheelchair, partnering with able-bodied men and women. And her company, Dancing Wheels, is the only professional group in the nation that mixes wheelchair-bound dancers with able-bodied dancers.

Mary was born with an extreme case of spina bifida. Her mother had been a professional dancer, working the various vaudeville circuits in the 1930s and 1940s. Her father was a pit orchestra musician. The couple was successful, famous on the circuit, and emotionally shattered by a daughter who, at best, would be confined to braces.

But Mary's desire to be a dancer was so intense that she tried to imitate the movements she saw her mother and her friends making. She was so determined that she regularly broke her leg braces, critical for her to stand erect and walk. Then, when she was ten, she twisted and turned so intensely while listening to the music that she shattered her legs. They healed in a way that can neither be corrected nor braced. She has been in a wheelchair ever since.

In theory there was no way Mary could become a dancer. Her parents, devastated by the experience, became overly protective, determined to help Mary with even the most intimate aspects of daily living. They attempted to suppress any ambitions she might have, hoping to keep her from injuring herself even more. Yet Mary had some friends sneak her to a parking lot where she could hear the music from a nearby bar, and she and a male friend attempted to dance. He moved his body gracefully, holding Mary's hands, her chair swaying. Then, on impulse, he spun her in the chair. To their surprise, the movement was graceful.

Mary and her friends began sneaking down to the

parking lot on a regular basis, practicing dancing. She also worked at home when she could, learning how to use her upper body in graceful movement, developing a dancer's skill from the waist up, as well as trying to discover how her chair could be effectively manipulated. When she and the young man who had been her first partner won a dance competition in which only able-bodied dancers competed, their work became serious. Mary realized that she could achieve her dream.

Mary faced setbacks along the way. When she wanted to be on her own, her parents became hostile to the idea. They feared her getting hurt, humiliating herself, being a failure. She left home anyway, aching over the estrangement, then was in an auto accident in her specially equipped van. It was only the fact that an able-bodied friend was riding with her as a passenger that she was able to escape the wreckage before the vehicle burst into flames. It was also the lowest emotional point Mary reached, convinced that perhaps her parents were right, that she was a fool to dream, to want to dance.

Yet Mary persisted. Although she has yet to be able to gain her parents' acceptance, perhaps the final stage of healing, she has achieved her dream. She has experienced the triumph of the human spirit through dance, certainly as miraculous a life healing as if her legs had been restored so she could walk.

God works in us, with us, and among us. Miracles, for such is how we define the normal events that we don't understand and can't duplicate, are happening constantly throughout the world. It is doubtful that any of us will ever see someone truly raised from the dead. We probably never will witness a person without a limb suddenly grow a new one. But whether the healing is a child's smile when a parent's soothing words end the fear that came from a nightmare, someone returning to an active life after having cancer surgery, or the peace and lack of fear on the face of the terminally ill just before death, the healing is of God and is a reflection of his unending love.

With all the cynicism that can exist in the healing field, the one truth is that whether or not our desired cures take place, healing is available to us all.

11

What Will You Do?

Faith healers have been around for a long time, and we're kidding ourselves if we expect them to go away. Our local newspapers will continue to tell us of their work, and we will continue to have our hopes and doubts. A suburban Chicago newspaper recently ran this Scripps Howard News Service story about a sixteen-year-old faith healer in Sweden.

> "I'm a perfectly ordinary girl," Samira Hannoch assures Swedish television viewers.
>
> But many people, convinced that she's anything but that, have pinned their last hopes on the 16-year-old.
>
> Thousands of ill people flock to Samira's hometown of Sodertalje, an hour's drive west of Stockholm, hoping that her hands will cure their ailments.
>
> Rumors about alleged miracle cures have spread far beyond Sweden, prompting people from Germany, Austria

and the United States to travel to Sweden so that she can touch their foreheads.

The phenomenon is highly unusual in a thoroughly Protestant country like Sweden, where people tend to take a sober-minded approach to life and generally aren't susceptible to apparitions.

The girl says monk Mar Chabel, revered as a saint by the Syrian orthodox church, appeared to her while she was watching TV at home last January. He asked her to settle a dispute among her church community, she says.

According to an earlier version, she saw an apparition of Jesus while she sat on the balcony. Samira and her aides now dismiss this version as wrong.

But she still maintains that following a second "revelation," oil—a symbol for the blood of Christ—flowed from her palms.

She now dips pieces of cotton wool into the oil she says flowed from her hands before she dabs people's foreheads.

In view of the overwhelming flow of people seeking her help, Samira's school principal has allowed her to stay away from classes until [the end of the school year].

Her classmates, unimpressed by her faith healing, are all negative in their comments.

In an interview with a national newspaper, they said Samira had always enjoyed playing the "prima donna" at school, driven by her desire to be at the center of attention. They said she had not hesitated to put on a real show to further her goal.

Now she really is at the center of attention. Long lines of sick and crippled people, among them many in wheelchairs, blind or carried on stretchers, wait their turn to receive her blessings in a local church building.

Generally, Samira's aides readily cooperate with the numerous reporters. However, if asked about any income from donations by their many visitors, they get tight-lipped.

During the total of three apparitions of her patron saint Mar Chabel, Samira said she was told what will happen to those who doubt her healing powers.

"Those who think that what you say is nothing but a silly girl's prattle will receive their punishment soon," she quotes him as telling her.

"Samira doesn't hesitate to describe the sort of punishment that will befall non-believers. They'll lose their eyesight, she says."[1]

What feelings and thoughts does this story, "Is Swedish Girl a Faith Healer, Or Just Seeking Attention?" elicit from you? Do you unreservedly believe the girl's healing power? Do you think the whole thing is a sham? What dynamics in this newspaper story remind you of things you've read in this book?

Put the story to some of the tests and questions this book has suggested.

- Is this kind of miracle possible?
- Could God use a sixteen-year-old girl to heal people?
- What is the healer's motive in pursuing her healing practices?
- Does the healer allow for medical verification of the healings?
- To whom does the healer give the credit for the healing?
- Does the healer acknowledge God's power?
- Does the healer call attention to herself?
- Does she accept that some people may not be healed by her touch?
- In what or in whom does the healer ask the ill people to place their faith?
- What about this healer is biblical?
- What about this healer is contrary to what we understand the Bible to say about healing?
- What appears to be the healer's purpose in healing other people?

- How seriously are the comments of the healer's peers to be taken?
- How seriously are the comments of the healed people to be taken?
- How do the threats that disbelief will lead to blindness make you feel about her as a healer?
- How does the mention of donations make you feel about the healer?
- Does the healer use methods that hint at fraud?
- What details of this story lead you to believe it's the story of a legitimate healer?
- What details of this story lead you to believe its the story of a fraudulent healer?
- What does this story do to the name of God?
- What does this story do to the name of other faith healers?

We obviously can't answer all of these questions from a short newspaper article, but these are the kinds of questions we should be asking, not only of this Swedish sixteen-year-old, but also of the faith healer who holds crusades in our town, of the television evangelist who heals people in front of the cameras, of the elder group that prays for the ill people in their church.

Having studied several thousand years of healing experiences, beliefs, practices, superstitions, and frauds, what conclusions can we reach? The first conclusion, and the important note of hope with which anyone studying this field must agree, is that God works miracles in our lives. Healing is both a natural part of the human condition and a gift of our Creator. But that healing does not routinely come through the almost magical showmanship of the professional faith healer. If anything, it occurs despite such occurrences. It happens many times a day throughout our lives, regardless of whether we are rich or poor, believers or nonbelievers, and no matter what our racial and ethnic heritage.

And the telling of those stories strengthens our faith. Each time we hear of a miraculous healing, we are both reminded of God's greatness and provided with hope for triumph over our own troubles. Such messages are perverted only when the messenger uses them for personal gain or glory, not for praise and hope.

Throughout this study I have been appalled by the abuses made in the name of God by individuals and religious organizations taking advantage of human misery to promote themselves. What can we do when we encounter such abuses? Is it enough to cluck our tongues and shake our heads? Or are we responsible to do something?

If Christians aren't willing to hold people accountable, the non-Christian media will be happy to expose the oddities and imbalances they see. On its August 21, 1992, broadcast, ABC's *20/20* exposed the cult-like practices of an extremist Christian group in Florida. As a result of the cult's practice to prohibit its members from using medical treatment, several children died from easily treatable conditions. Situations like this damage the name of faith healing, the name of the Christian church, and ultimately the name of God.

The body of faith should take responsibility to monitor its own. I hope this book becomes a call to action, a call to healthy skepticism, and a desire to maintain the purity of the church's witness.

DISCERNING FAITH FROM FRAUD

It is only human for us to worry about our relationship with God. We sometimes wonder whether others might not be serving God more or better than we are, or perhaps their prayers are more effective than ours. The problem is that fraudulent faith healers are able to prey upon such insecurities that most of us experience from time to time. If the healer's healings are ineffective, he or she can always claim that we simply lacked faith.

In the United States, we have by legal means kept religion apart from the affairs of government, which is beneficial on the whole, but it means that governmental bodies are largely unwilling to legislate what is good or bad for people when it comes to their religious beliefs. We have little recourse if we fall victim to those who falsely claim to heal in the name of Christ. In a legal sense, it is no different that any other poor medical choice we might make—except that bad faith healers cannot be sued for malpractice. There is no law against following such faith healers or using prayer rather than medicine. The First Amendment protects us from extremists who want us to worship in only one way—their way—but it also assures that religious frauds may continue working as long as people flock to them.

The vast majority of the religions practiced in the U.S.—including most Christian denominations—allow for and accept the use of conventional medicine, viewing it as another valuable tool of God. Most religious leaders feel that knowledge of pharmaceuticals, surgery, psychology, and other forms of treatment are all gifts of God. They can be misused, of course, as can any of the other gifts of the Creator. But what matters is that, according to most beliefs, there need be no limits to the various methods of healing. Much conventional medical practice has even begun to acknowledge that the whole person—body, mind, and spirit—is critical for healing, longevity, and quality of life.

There are documented cases of individuals experiencing spontaneous remissions of their illness—in cases, immediately after praying for such a healing. Often such prayers were private, between the sufferer and God. At other times friends or fellow church members had prayed for the ill person. Sometimes the person had attended a healing service.

It is, of course, conceivable that God could choose to heal a sick person through the "unlikely vessel" of a sincere but ineffective faith healer—or even through a faith healer who may actually be trying to con people out of their money. Still, however, offering hope to the seemingly hopeless is a cruel yet not unusual activity for the dishonest.

So how do we discern faith from fraud?

First of all, never forget that God is the only healer. Jesus stressed that fact again and again.

Also recognize that healing comes in many forms. Yes, God can work any miracle he wants. God can make an old person young and a young person old. He can heal cancer. He can make the blind see, the lame walk, and restore hearing to the deaf. Literally all things are possible with God. Yet many times healing means the acceptance of an irreversible physical condition. Sometimes healing comes through a peaceful death, a passing on to the next stage of existence in our eternal relationship with our Lord.

No one is more valuable to God simply because that person has been physically restored to good health; nor is someone lacking in God's love merely because that person continues to endure deformity, chronic illness, or some other affliction. God's love is a given. His ways are often a mystery in this life. Since the good may suffer and the bad may not, it is important that you not try to judge healing in human terms. It is not for us to decide what criteria God must meet when we or our loved ones seek the Creator's healing.

A member of the clergy, a faith healer, or anyone else engaging in healing has no right to determine precisely what end God intends for us. Intercessory prayer can be valuable. Personal prayer can be valuable. Joining with friends to petition God through prayer can be valuable. And we have no reason *not* to expect a miracle. But none of us has the wisdom to discern what form that healing will be or should be. I find those who regularly claim to offer consistent, definite results through their work as God's "vehicle" (or "intermediary" or "specially anointed one" or whatever other phrase they use) to be either outright frauds or suffering from delusions.

I am especially appalled by those who try to convince the sufferers that if healing does not occur through the healer's own efforts, then the problem is the sufferer's lack of faith. Was Job unfaithful? What about Moses, whose speech impediment was never healed, who needed Aaron to help him communicate, yet who led God's people to the promised land? What about the mysterious thorn in Paul's flesh—very likely some physical ailment that God decided not to remove? The idea of the "unlikely vessel" is repeated again and again throughout the Bible.

In our time you need only think of the dynamic Christian testimonies of such people as Bob Weiland (who lost both legs in Vietnam) or Joni Earickson Tada (who is a quadriplegic), both of whom have built powerful outreach ministries in spite of the fact that God's healing in their lives has not included physical restoration. Do they lack faith? Would any faith healer dare say that God has refused to heal Joni because of some unacknowledged disobedience to God in her life?

So what is the answer?

First, recognize that all healing comes from God and that there is no single way to be healed. If you are obese, healing may come from your decision to change your diet and to exercise more, God giving you the strength to stay with a regimen that will restore your health. If you need surgery, your healing may come from God's gift of knowledgeable, skilled surgeons who will physically correct the problem. The nurse who comforts and cares for you, the therapist who helps you regain lost skills, and even the orderlies who assist with your most basic of bodily functions all are living out Christ's admonition to love others as oneself. God can use all of them in healing. You are not lacking in faith when you seek the aid of professionals trained in the medical sciences; you are, rather, recognizing God's loving power that is being passed through others to you.

Second, do not deny the power of personal and communal prayer. Ask God to heal you. Request the prayers of others. The issue of why you are in ill health does not alter his responsiveness. God's timing may not match your desires, but prayer speeds healing and shows respect and awe for God's continued involvement in all aspects of our lives.

Third, do not put your faith in a person who claims to have "the answer" to what ails you. Healing is effected in many ways, but I have yet to see a full-time professional faith healer who is capable of *routinely* helping a person to the degree possible with traditional medicine and/or psycho-therapy when used alongside prayer. In some instances, delaying the use of doctors to whom God has imparted healing wisdom can mean needless suffering or early death. Ultimately, it is foolish not to combine the best physical, psychological, and spiritual care available to you.

Do not challenge God by defining exactly how you expect a healing to take place. Faith healers seldom restore mobility to the limbs of the chronically crippled, sight to the blind whose eyes have been severely damaged, or hearing to the long-term deaf. Honest healers know that true healing may be nothing more than recovering a long-lost inner peace, enabling the sufferer to endure affliction or have the courage to continue to pursue physical or psychological health. Dishonest healers may attack your faith in God, asserting that he always fully cures the physical illnesses of the faithful. A continuing serious heart condition, for instance, would be viewed as your not being right with God. That is an inexcusable accusation—especially for someone with heart problems!

Recognize that there is nothing sinful about being disabled, in ill health, or otherwise physically limited. Nowhere does Jesus say that God's wrath comes in the form of influenza, colds, cancer, a cleft palate, a deformed back, multiple sclerosis, heart disease, or any other illness or physical affliction. By the same token, however, it is not a sin against God to try to be restored to full health, to end a disability, or to pray and take action to improve one's condition.

Finally, remember that Jesus never asked for money in return for healing. He never put a monetary value on receiving God's power. The Lord's Prayer does not require a donation each time it is prayed.

Spiritual healers who demand money for their services are unlikely to be God's vehicles. Physicians do, of course, charge fees and have always received payment for their services. It is likely that Luke, believed to have been both a physician and the author of the books of Luke and Acts, charged for his skills as a doctor. But while the Bible makes clear that certain people traveling with Jesus raised funds to cover the cost of their travels (Judas was the treasurer!), such donations were never connected with healing services. A doctor who charges for healing is acting according to accepted social custom and relies on such fees to provide for his or her family and continuing education. But a faith healer who charges as a prerequisite for spiritual healing services is at best misrepresenting God's love, and at worst, a complete fraud.

While each healer is different, there are some tests you can apply:

1. Faith healing must not be based on financial support.

Although it is possible that a legitimate spiritual healer might charge a fixed admission fee to a healing service, it is more likely that a legitimate healer will ask only for a voluntary donation.

2. Healers are not substitutes for trained medical professionals. Nor are healers easy alternatives to basic, sensible health habits. Distrust healers who do not expect you to change self-destructive habits in order to be well. Distrust healers who forbid you from seeking medical or psychological help along with the spiritual, or who recommend you not seek other spiritual counsel, from a local pastor, for instance. Be especially distrustful of those who say that to utilize conventional medicine is to lack faith in God.

3. ~~God heals where, when, and how he chooses~~. Faith can heal you, but remember that many people also experience healing who do not know God or who deny him completely. God's love is not given based on our own human standards. Likewise, what constitutes God's healing for us may not be exactly what we desire as humans. There are quadriplegics who feel healed by God despite their limitations. Most of us want physical healing rather than spiritual healing, yet the latter is often the greater gift of the Lord. Again, avoid those healers who try to impose their standards.

4. Legitimate faith healers make no guarantees, do not imply they will be successful, or otherwise raise false hopes.

5. Legitimate faith healers are comfortable with you using your own internal spiritual resources, relying upon your own relationship with God as well as the relationship you have within the community of believers. Someone who teaches you to pray for healing yourself may be a more legitimate healer than someone who insists you pray during his or her healing service.

6. Be wary of the healer who seems more concerned

with putting on a show for the faithful than with helping you. Many healers even refuse to meet with anyone outside of their televised or broadcast healing services. They will not come to your home. They will not meet with you privately in their office. There is dramatic excitement to the laying on of hands in a gathering of hundreds or thousands of the faithful, but there should be just as much love, just as much healing power, in a quiet prayer spoken over the telephone when you are too sick to attend the service.

7. Be wary of traveling healers who come to town, seem to heal a few people in a dramatic service, then go on to the next community. They can say whatever they want to get you to the tent, church, hall, or auditorium. They can proclaim whatever "miracles" they feel they can get away with. And when the emotional excitement is over, when you are in a position to seek medical confirmation of the healing, they do not have to answer for their false claims. They are long gone.

This does not mean that established local healers won't make exaggerated claims or state outright lies as well. It just means that they are more likely to have to be accountable for their actions, and thus more likely to act with honesty and integrity.

8. Be wary of the sincere individual who makes outrageous claims of personal power. The most legitimate faith healers are also the most humble of human beings.

Remember, any of us can heal others in the name of the Lord. That is one of Jesus' promises to us. But when it happens, when our words heal a heart or our hands heal a body, there is an overwhelming humility experienced by most people. For one brief moment we are intensely, miraculously, and joyfully the conduit for God's healing power. We are simultaneously brought close to other humans and to our Creator. We are both a part of and a witness to what, for humans, is a miracle. The bragging, self-centered "healer," who makes lots of claims about his or her successes, is more likely to be a fraud than to be someone who is a conduit for God's healing power.

9. Finally, be wary of the healer who does not also encourage you to pursue all paths available to you. Most legitimate healers, including ministers who hold healing services, encourage the full use of medical, psychological, and spiritual help. Prayer may make surgery or medication unnecessary, or it may speed the healing. But legitimate healers will not tell you to stop seeing a physician. They know that sometimes you need all knowledge God has given to humans, and when you don't, the visit to the doctor simply confirms the blessing.

HOLDING HEALERS ACCOUNTABLE

What happens when a professional healer's actions fail to help someone who is sick? What happens when a healer's admonitions concerning faith cause someone with a serious illness to stop other forms of treatment, dying needlessly? What happens when someone who knows they have no special healing ability claims to be a spiritual treater of illness? And what about the itinerant healer, moving from town to town, healing the sick, calling out spirits, commanding the lame to walk, and then moving on before the "miracles" can be evaluated?

In most instances, the answer is nothing. The laws that assure our freedom of religion also place the responsibility for our religious mistakes on us. The courts have generally held that it is better for the public to have problems with the occasional fraudulent religious leader than to say what is proper or improper religious practice.

In rare cases, a healer crosses over the line between practicing faith healing and practicing medicine without a license. A few faith healers have actually committed crimes that made them vulnerable to legal action. Occasionally, a faith healer has even been prosecuted for extortion for subtly implying that good health is determined by the amount of money contributed to his or her ministry.

But by and large it is extrememly difficult to determine the intention and attitude of the healer when considering civil or criminal charges. Is the person sincere? Misguided? Delusional? Deliberately dishonest? And how do you actually prove it?

The result of such confusion is that there is seldom any recourse against a fraudulent faith healer. Instead, our best protection comes from being actively involved in a community of Christian believers with whom we are comfortable. This might be a national healing organization such as the Order of St. Luke. Or it might be our local church where the pastor and the congregation form a loving "home."

Praying with a friend, being placed on a prayer list used by members of the church, or the healing ministration of the pastor all are positive actions for healing. There are few, if any, unrealistic expectations. Furthermore, in a community of loving believers we can be accountable to each other.

Accountability does not exist with itinerant healers, television preachers, and the like. In a local church there is more opportunity to coordinate all the various channels of treatment for illness. The sufferer can be with family and loved ones, seek trusted medical professionals, and share the love of other Christians. The environment for healing is enhanced, the problems of possible fraud either eliminated or so minimal as to be of almost no concern.

Notes

Chapter 2—The Healers

[1]The need to anoint with oil was not universally practiced by the early church. While other aspects of the healing work of the elders and others can be found consistently, the anointing in the name of the Lord occurs only in James and Mark 6:13—"They drove out many demons and anointed many sick people with oil and healed them."

[2]Oral Roberts, *Your Road to Recovery* (Nashville: Oliver Nelson, 1986), 42–43.

[3]Ernest Angley, *Faith in God Heals the Sick* (Akron, Ohio: Winston Press, 1983), 62–63.

[4]Ibid., 62.

[5]Ibid., 34–35.

[6]Ibid., 35.

[7]It's important to differentiate between Roberts the fund raiser and Roberts the healer. The language and seeming attitude are often quite different for each. Historically, a number of evangelists have used the concept of personal death to raise money or impress their followers. Some evangelists imply that death will be a punishment for failure, an odd concept for Christians, who generally believe in a better life to come. Other evangelists imply that they are alive to accomplish certain goals. When they are no longer effective, it's time to move on to a new stage of existence. Ironically, even though men like Oral Roberts speak joyously of the world to come, some have been known to fight for life at all costs, urging their followers to save them by making contributions to their ministries. But Roberts' method of claiming that unless a large sum

of money is raised "God will call me home" should not bias the observer from looking at other aspects of the man's teachings.

[8]Kathryn Kuhlman, *I Believe in Miracles* (Englewood Cliffs, N.J.: Prentice-Hall, 1962).

[9]Ibid. See the story of Bruce Baker and specifically pages 54–55.

[10]Ibid. See especially pages 95–98. Of importance when discussing Kuhlman's presentation of the healing is the paragraph on page 97 that reads:

"Mary had now been going to the services for several months, and although spiritually she was vastly improved, her physical condition seemed to be growing steadily worse. Her breathlessness had increased to the point where she could scarcely walk even on a level. It was becoming increasingly difficult for her to swallow, and her eating was already greatly restricted. She knew if God did not heal her, she would undoubtedly die from the goiter, as had her mother and aunt before her, from the same affliction."

In this instance, however, she returned to a Kuhlman healing service in May 1949; the goiter was miraculously cured despite not being touched by Kuhlman. Mary turned in a prayer request to the healer, but she did not meet her on stage, nor was she addressed in the audience. She simply lost the goiter, spending three sleepless nights before returning to her doctor who confirmed the healing (98). See also George Bishop, *Faith Healing: God or Fraud?* (Los Angeles: Sherbourne Press, 1967), 59–73.

Chapter 3—The Fraudulent Healer

[1]James Randi, *Flim Flam* (Buffalo, N.Y.: Prometheus Books, 1982).

[2]Ibid., 204.

[3]Ibid., 207.

[4]Ibid., 204–9.

[5]James Randi, *The Faith Healers* (Buffalo, N.Y.: Prometheus Books, 1989), 100.

[6]Ibid.

[7]Ibid., 105–6.

[8]Ibid., 104–5.

[9]Ibid., 20–30. See also: Ruth Cranston, *The Miracle of Lourdes* (New York: McGraw-Hill, 1955); Patrick Marnham, *Lourdes: A Modern Pilgrimage* (New York: Coward, McCann & Geoghegan, 1981); and Donald Sharkey, *After Bernadette: The Story of Modern Lourdes* (Milwaukee: The Bruce Publishing Co., 1945).

CHAPTER 4—Healing, Faith, and Prayer

[1]J. B. Phillips, *The Price of Success* (Wheaton, Ill.: Harold Shaw, 1984), 112–4.

[2]From a personal interview.

[3]There is extensive controversy over the issue of whether a lack of faith affects a physical healing. One of the Biblical passages noted is Mark 5:28–35, the story of the woman who touches Jesus' clothing when seeking a healing. Jesus tells her that her faith has caused the healing.

Many contemporary religious scholars say that the importance of the passage is that Jesus was speaking against the talismans of the healing magicians among the Jews and the pagans. These magicians would often claim that clothing and other items they had worn, touched, or otherwise blessed had magic powers. Jesus, by contrast, wanted to make clear that he was healing through God's power; it was not the touch of his clothing that caused the healing.

The theologians who stress God's healing in this story generally do not feel that it's accurate to say that the opposite to the idea is true. That is, that if the woman lacked faith, God would not have healed her. The point seems to be that healing comes from God and through God, not any individual or talisman. The issue was whether the healing was by magic or faith, not whether or not God would withhold his healing if she had not had "adequate" faith.

[4]According to Dr. Byrd, "It was assumed that some of the patients in both groups would be prayed for by people not associated with the study; this was not controlled for. Thus some of the patients in the control group would be prayed for, whereas all of the patients in the prayer group would be (i.e., by both non-associated people and by the designated intercessors of the study)."

He also explained: "Several points concerning the present study should be mentioned. First, prayer by and for the control group (by persons not in conjunction with this study) could not be accounted for. Nor was there any attempt to limit prayer among the controls. Such action would certainly be unethical and probably impossible to achieve. Therefore, 'pure' groups were not attained in this study—all of one group and part of the other had access to the intervention under study. This may have resulted in smaller differences observed between the two groups. How God acted in this situation is unknown; i.e., were the groups treated by God as a whole or were individual prayers alone answered? Second, whether patients prayed of themselves and to what degree they held religious convictions was not determined. Because many of the patients were seriously ill, it was not possible to obtain an interview extensive enough to answer these two questions. Furthermore, it was thought that discussions concerning the patients' relationship to God might be emotionally disturbing to a significant number of patients at the time of admission to the coronary care unit, though it was generally noted that almost all patients in the study expressed the belief that prayer probably helped and certainly could not hurt."

There are other variables that were not addressed and must be mentioned for the sake of accuracy. For example, were members of the group that healed faster in better health, at least in terms of previous diet and exercise? Did they come from a loving, supportive home environment? Did they feel that they had a reason to live or had they come to the hospital thinking that all their major accomplishments were behind them, that it did not matter whether they lived or died? Did they have unfinished goals that made recovery important to them?

What about diet within the hospital? Did they use vitamin supplements? Did they choose to eat a healthier variety of foods than those in the control group?

All such circumstances could have an impact on the results. What is important, though, is the size of the sample. The numbers were large enough that even with these variables unaccounted for, the results should not be much different than if all factors were considered before the participants were randomly divided by the computer.

Chapter 5—Illness and Demonic Influence

[1]This belief was used to explain why early humans were often frightened of the solitude of the desert. Rather than accepting the idea that the desert was an intensely lonely place and that individuals were not meant to live in such isolation, Azazel was blamed. Many travelers took offerings to Azazel as a way of protecting themselves against an unexpected encounter.

[2]Among the resources for this information, refer to: Duane Empey and Ted Schwarz, *Satanism: Is Your Family Safe?* (Grand Rapids: Zondervan, 1988); Rosemary Guiley, *Encyclopedia of Witches and Witchcraft* (New York: Facts on File, 1989); Madeleine S. Miller and J. Lane , *The New Harper's Bible Dictionary* (New York: Harper & Row, 1973); Rossell Hope Robbins, *Encyclopedia of Witchcraft and Demonology* (New York: Bonanza Books, 1981); and Jeffrey Burton Russell, *The Devil: Perceptions of Evil from Antiquity to Primitive Christianity* (Ithaca, N.Y.: Cornell University Press, 1977).

[3]See note 2.

[4]See note 2.

[5]In our English translations of the Bible, the words "demon," "Satan," and "devil" seem to be interchangeable. In the original languages, however, the meanings of these words varied. When the third-century Egyptian Jews translated the Old Testament into Greek, they used the word *diabolos*. The term meant an angel whose job was to test human faithfulness to God. *Diabolos* was not evil, though his actions upset those humans who were found to be unfaithful. *Diabolos* presented humans with a choice, letting their free will determine how God would view them for their actions, yet remaining neutral in the choices they made.

The New Testament uses the term *diabolus* as Satan, the adversary who hates humanity and wants to destroy men and women, estranging them from God. Only as the translations evolved did readers come to see demons as totally evil, as forms of Satan or his underlings.

[6]From personal interviews.

[7]From personal interviews.

[8]From personal interviews.

[9]From personal interviews.

[10]From personal interviews.

[11]From my own personal experiences during the research for this book. Also, James Randi mentions these in his books, and there are regular advertisements for this type of healing in such tabloids as the *National Enquirer.*

[12]These fringe groups are usually small store-front type operations, as well as mid-size churches, usually non-denominational, found throughout the country. I have frequently talked with them when on tour for my own books, especially those relating to abnormal psychology such as hysteric dissociation (multiple personality).

[13]Based on several newspaper stories reported in Arizona, Texas, and California.

[14]Based on interviews conducted for articles for *Family Circle, The Akron Beacon Journal, The Flagstaff Times,* and other periodicals.

[15]See note 14.

[16]"Dost thou renounce the devil and all his works, the vain pomp and glory of the world, with all covetous desires of the same, and the sinful desires of the flesh, so that thou wilt not follow, nor be led by them?"

"Answer: I renounce them all; and, by God's help, will endeavour not to follow, nor be led by them." From the rite of adult baptism, *The Book of Common Prayer and Administration of the Sacraments and Other Rites and Ceremonies of the Church,* according to the use of the Protestant

Episcopal Church in the United States (Greenwich, Conn.: Seabury Press, 1952).

[17]From personal interview.

[18]From personal interview.

[19]From personal interviews.

Chapter 6—Healing Practices in Biblical Times

[1]Abraham Cohen, *Everyman's Talmud* (New York: Schocken Books, 1975), 241.

[2]Ibid., 242.

[3]Ibid., 243. See also Ben Zion Bokser, translator, *The Talmud: Selected Writings* (New York: Paulist Press, 1989), 48.

[4]Cohen, *Everyman's Talmud*, 246.

[5]Ibid., 247.

[6]Miller and Lane, *The New Harper's Bible Dictionary*.

[7]Cohen, *Everyman's Talmud*, 250–59.

[8]Ibid., 248.

[9]Ibid., 252. The people believed that God frequently reveals both himself and his will through flames; thus the person doing the healing is asking that God be present as the ritual is taking place. *Shechinah* is a term used to explain the manifestation of God in the world. The literal translation is "dwelling," but the meaning was more in line with radiance. One explanation is that the Shechinah is the "face of God" as seen on earth. Just as we experience daylight, which is the illumination of earth by the sun, so we experience the Shechinah, the radiance of God in heaven on earth. The Shechinah is present everywhere. The presence is more intense under certain circumstances, however, such as with Moses and the burning bush, as well as in especially holy locations.

[10]Ibid., 255.

[11]Ibid., 256.

[12]Ibid., 251–52.

[13]From interviews with members of the cancer research center at University of Arizona Medical Center. Similar comments were made by researchers during unrelated interviews at the University of Pittsburgh Medical Center and Children's Hospital.

[14]Cohen, *Everyman's Talmud*, 205.

[15]Spittle was believed to cause a chemical reaction with certain foods popular in areas where the superstition of spittle as healing or curative came about. Whether or not the use of spittle for eye problems evolved from this or something else has not been found in research to date.

Chapter 7—The Healing Touch

[1]The historical data and anecdotes in the first half of this chapter were largely adapted from a number of historical sources and secondary references: Edward Law Hussey, "On the Cure of Scrofulous Diseases Attributed to the Royal Touch," *Archaeological Journal,* vol. x (1855), 187–211, 377; Cornelius Nicholls, "Touching for the King's Evil," *Home Counties Magazine* (England), vol. xiv (1912), 112–122; "A Touchpiece of Henry IX," *The Numismatist* (March 1912); Raymond Henry Crawford, *The King's Evil* (Oxford: The Clarendon Press, 1911); George Bishop, *Faith Healing: God or Fraud?* (Los Angeles: Sherbourne Press, 1967), 46, 226; William Andrews, *Historical Romance: Strange Stories, Characters, Scenes, Mysteries, Memorable Events, in the History of Old England* (London: Hamilton, Adams and Co., 1883).

[2]Currently one of the best books on therapeutic touch as utilized by members of the medical profession in conjunction with other treatment is Janet Macrae, *Therapeutic Touch: A Practical Guide* (New York: Knopf, 1988).

[3]Interviews with Dolores Krieger, R.N., Ph.D., retired, and members of the staff of New York University's graduate course on therapeutic touch.

[4]See previous note.

[5]Interviews with Dr. Norman Harris whose Harris method of birthing has long been used by hospitals throughout the world, and whose PMS program is currently in use in several clinics throughout the United States.

Chapter 8—Mesmer and Christian Science

[1]See also Stefan Zweig, *Mental Healers: Franz Anton Mesmer, Mary Baker Eddy, Sigmund Freud* (Garden City, N.Y.: Garden City Publishing, 1934); George Bishop, *Faith Healing: God or Fraud?* (Los Angeles: Sherbourne Press, 1967).

[2]Benjamin Franklin, *The Writings of Benjamin Franklin,* ed. Albert Henry Smyth (New York: Macmillan Company, 1907), vol. IX.

[3]Carl Van Doren, *Benjamin Franklin* (Garden City, N.Y.: Garden City Publishing, 1938), 713–17.

[4]Earl Schipper, *Cults in North America* (Grand Rapids: Christian Schools International, 1987), 96.

[5]Mary Baker Eddy, *Science and Health with Key to the Scriptures* (Boston: Published by the trustees under the will of Mary Baker Eddy, 1875), 394–5.

[6]Mary Baker Eddy, *Science and Health with Key to the Scriptures* (Boston: The First Church of Christ, Scientist, 1971).

[7]Ibid.

[8]Schipper, *Cults in North America,* 108.

[9]Mary Baker Eddy, *Science and Health with Key to the Scriptures* (Boston: Published by the trustees under the will of Mary Baker Eddy, 1906).

[10]Based on a case study in Schipper, *Cults in North America,* 118.

[11]Mary Baker Eddy, *Christian Healing* (Boston: Published by the trustees under the will of Mary Baker Eddy, 1886, 1908, 1914).

[12]Eddy, *Science and Health,* (1906).

[13]Bishop, *Faith Healing,* 160–73.

[14]George Channing, as quoted in *Religions in America,* ed. Leo Rosten (New York: Simon and Schuster, 1963), 45.

[15]The autopsy revealed that the cause of death was bacterial meningitis, an inflammation of the membranes surrounding the brain and spinal cord. Children who receive massive doses of intravenous antibiotics for bacterial meningitis almost always recover. Many of them, however, are left with brain damage from the illness. More important for Seth Glaser, the time between when it became obvious that he was in trouble and his death, a time when the parents were expected to take him to a doctor if they followed traditional medical practices, was just thirty hours.

[16]Information on the Glaser case, including the transcript of the quote, was provided by the First Church of Christ Scientist Committee on Publications. Nathan Talbot of the Church was present during the questioning by Los Angeles Police Detective Richard Cooper. The same records are available to the public through the Los Angeles County court system, the hearing having been held in December 1989.

[17]See previous note.

[18]Eddy, *Science and Health,* 237:15–22.

[19]Channing, quoted in *Religions in America,* ed. Rosten, 47.

[20]Ibid.

Chapter 9—The Merging of the Church and Medicine

[1]S. I. McMillen, *None of These Diseases* (Old Tappan, N.J.: Revell, 1977), 14–15.

[2]Patent medicine involved the use of non-prescription liquids, poultices, herbs, and other potions. The majority of the products contained alcohol in fairly large quantity. Being drunk eased the pain, and imbibing on patent medicine was far more respectable than going into a bar. Otherwise temperate people often had a potent bottle of an over-the-counter medication readily at hand.

[3]The information in the rest of this chapter was drawn from a variety of sources, primarily: Guy Williams, *The Age of Agony: The Art of Healing, 1700–1800* (Chicago: Academy Chicago Publishers, 1986); Guy Williams, *The Age of Miracles: Medicine and Surgery in the Nineteenth Century* (Chicago: Academy Chicago Publishers, 1987); Charles Panati, *Breakthrough: Astonishing Advances in Your Lifetime in Medicine, Science, and Technology* (New York: Houghton Mifflin, 1980); Samuel Hopkins Adams, *The Great American Fraud* (New York: P. F. Collier & Son, 1907); Adelaide Hechtlinger, *The Great Patent Medicine Era—Or, Without Benefit of Doctor* (New York: Grosset & Dunlap, 1970); and Laurence Johnson, *Over the Counter and On the Shelf: Country Storekeeping in America, 1620–1920* (New York: Bonanza Books, 1961).

Chapter 10—Health and Wholeness

[1]Lisa F. Berkman and Lester Breslow, *Health and Ways of Living: The Alameda County Study* (New York: Oxford University Press, 1983).

[2]The example is apocryphal. The facts are based on research by Dr. John Kappas of Van Nuys, California, who was interviewed for this book, and the book by Emrikus Padus, *The Complete Guide to Your Emotions and Your Health* (Emmaus, Pennsylvania: Rodale, 1986).

[3]See previous note.

[4]Berkman and Breslow, *Health and Ways of Living*.

[5]From interviews with researcher Dr. Bernard Green, pediatrics expert Dr. Richard Martin, and others, and from the book by Alan Beck and Aaron Katcher, *Between Pets and People: The Importance of Animal Companionship* (New York: Putnam, 1984). See also Padus, *The Complete Guide to Your Emotions and Your Health*, 656–62.

[6]Also see Beck and Katcher's *Between Pets and People* (see previous note). Although no longer in print at this writing, your library should be able to locate a copy for you to read. The research reported has been consistently supported by other institutions.

[7]Bernard Siegel, M.D., as quoted in *The Complete Guide to Your Emotions and Your Health*, 528–42.

Chapter 11—What Will You Do?

[1]Thomas Borchert, "Is Swedish Girl a Faith Healer, Or Just Seeking Attention?" © 1992 by Deutsche Presse Agentur (dpa) 1992. Used with permission.